THE LIVING WORKPLACE

www.thelivingworkplace.com

Ann Coombs

with Marion E. Raycheba

The Living Workplace

Soul, Spirit,
and Success
in the
21st Century

 HarperBusiness
HarperCollins*PublishersLtd*

The Living Workplace:
Soul, Spirit and Success in the 21st Century
Copyright © 2001 by Ann Coombs.
All rights reserved. No part of this book may be
used or reproduced in any manner whatsoever
without prior written permission except in the
case of brief quotations embodied in reviews.
For information address
HarperCollins Publishers Ltd.,
55 Avenue Road, Suite 2900,
Toronto, Ontario, Canada M5R 3L2

www.harpercanada.com

HarperCollins books may be purchased for educa-
tional, business, or sales promotional use.
For information please write:
Special Markets Department,
HarperCollins Canada,
55 Avenue Road, Suite 2900,
Toronto, Ontario, Canada M5R 3L2

First trade paper edition

Excerpt from *Repair of the World* is reprinted
by permission of the author. Copyright Naomi
Newman, April 1994.

"Comparing Theories of Change," by Michael
Beer and Nitia Nohria, is from "Cracking the
Code of Change" in the May/June 2000 issue of
the *Harvard Business Review*. It is reproduced
here by kind permission of Harvard Business
School Publishing.

"What the Boss Needs to Know," by Patricia
Chisholm, appeared in the May 29, 2000, issue of
Maclean's magazine. It is reproduced here by kind
permission of *Maclean's*.

Canadian Cataloguing in Publication Data

Coombs, Ann
The living workplace : soul, spirit and success in
the 21st century

Includes index.
ISBN 0-00-638569-9

1. Work – Religious aspects.
2. Quality of work life.
3. Spiritual life.
I. Title.

BL65.W67C66 2002   291.1'785   C2001-902541-6

HC 9 8 7 6 5 4 3 2 1

Printed and bound in the United States
Set in Aldus

For my Father

In every moment with every act
We can heal our world and us.
We are all holy sparks dulled by separation.
When we work
With holiness in our eyes
Our brokenness will end

Repair of the World:
A Kabbalistic Creation Story
Written by Naomi Newman
Based on a creation myth
by Rabbi Isaac Luria (1488–1575)

Contents

Chapter 1: Future Zone   [3]

What will be the realities of the future workplace? How will these realities affect workers and employers, and how will we perceive, understand and undertake the role of work? The balance of power between employers and employees is shifting. What will success look like? How will it be measured? Who will succeed, and who will not?

Chapter 2: Truth & Consequences   [26]

How is truth defined in today's workplace? How is truth related to ethics? How do we understand ethics and ethical standards? How do we express them in workplace behaviors? What happens when our personal values and standards—our concept of truth and how it should be expressed—are at variance with what we find in the workplace?

Chapter 3: The Toxic Workplace [43]

What is a toxic workplace? How does it affect workers' lives, relationships and health? Can we find a solution that will alleviate the pain, confusion and anxiety that result from working in a toxic environment?

Chapter 4: Winds of Change [65]

What is involved in dealing with change, living with uncertainty, accepting change and creating change?

Chapter 5: Name That Fear [91]

How does fear change us? What price do we pay within our souls? How can we pull ourselves free from the force of fear?

Chapter 6: Say, Listen, Hear [106]

What will be the language of the living workplace? What roles will trust, sharing and openness play in communications? What effect will the new language have on corporate success and survival?

Chapter 7: The Spiritual Worker [125]

Is it reasonable to expect an employer to provide spiritual nourishment to employees? What are the consequences for corporations and their employees if the workplace is not spiritually sustaining? What choices are workers making when they realize their workplace environments are not spiritually nourishing?

Chapter 8: The Passionate Heart   [150]

How are entrepreneurs finding their way? What is the source of their courage? What are the qualities they need to bring their dreams to life? What does living in a fully engaged way mean? What is the role of the passionate heart?

Acknowledgments

There are so many who have profoundly affected my life's journey and been part of moments that will remain forever etched in my mind and soul.

First, Dr. Harry Robinson, whose faith and friendship have been the greatest inspiration.

David Short, Edie Rittenger, Ruth Matheson, Paula Thomas and Janet Anderson for their continued generosity and kindness. Their knowledge and invincible faith are a testimony for many.

Sir John Templeton and Joanna Hill of The Templeton Foundation, whose time, letters and guidance are deeply appreciated.

Michael and Elaine Pountney, who shared hours with me in debate, interviews and encouragement. I continue to hold them in the highest regard.

I have been blessed with family always generous with love, support, encouragement, patience, understanding and knowing. My mother understood the challenge from the beginning. My brothers, John and Chip, give me great joy by sharing their lives. My beloved cousins, Susan Goodall, Jane Needles, Margot MacLaren and Susan Meisner, all gave me endless support.

True and forgiving friendship is a gift. I count these individuals among the most valuable gifts in my life: Renee FitzGerald, Jennifer Burke, Sandra Millar, Suzanne Bolton, Jacqueline Jamieson, Kathleen Barber, Barbara Griffiths, Barbara Assaf, Peter and Brenda Hochachka, Joe and Diane Bishop, Barbara Raphael, Lennie Kronisch, Sandy Teufel, Karen Petach, Rita Morin, Jean Barton, Elizabeth Ball, Hazel White, Joseph Duggan, Angela Wattie, Georgia Taylor, Lyn Gaby, Patty Crosbie, Tony and Susan Barrett, Dr. Roger Rogers, Laura Corobotic, Judy Davis, Joanne Fallow, Barbara MacPherson, Georgina Montgomery, Karl and Nora Stittgen, Bruce Burnett, Jill Justice, Lee and Fraser Lindsay and Shelley Easthope, Julia Zen Zen, Lynne and Gerry Kennedy, Richard Mew, Lama Zopa and Sherry Eaton.

In my work, there are many to thank for their support and encouragement: Megan Kennedy, Ivan de Lorenzana, Lisa Tant, Susan Cohen, Vicki Haller, James Terry, Scott McRae, Susan Johnston, Karin Maier, Catherine Sleep, Jean Pierre Challet, John Fowles, Wayne Stafford, Kelly Cunningham, Nancy Redner, Nada Ristich, Alison Youngman and Scott Jolliffe, and forever loyal Sherri Slobodian.

There have been many throughout my career who helped me prepare for this book: Don Hudson, Bill McCourt, Jeff Mooney, Dr. Fred Fry, Rick Griffiths, and hundreds of clients are among them.

My gratitude also goes to all who helped with research, advice, thoughts and suggestions. Special thanks to Marilyn Knox and Joseph Coates, whom I hold in high regard.

Warmest thanks to Judy Brunsek and Don Loney of Harper-Collins Canada Ltd., who believed in me and this book from the beginning, and to Nicole Langlois whose brilliant editing was done with care.

The journey continues to be one of learning and loving.

ANN COOMBS
SPRING 2002

Foreword

*W*ork can be defined in so many ways: employment, occupation, task, labor, toil. A minister friend once said to me that we are here to work out our soul's destiny, and the work we do can be simply an avenue through which this may be accomplished. If we keep poised and balanced, doing our best every day, realizing that under all circumstances it is important to be compassionate, kind and generous with those we meet on life's journey—if we continue doing our best work and thinking our best thoughts every day—we can gradually wear away concerns over problems.

There seems to be a simplicity in what we seek to do when we dedicate ourselves to the doing. When we choose to accept into our consciousness only what uplifts, but do not reject that which we may not understand, we do things that need to be done in a more loving state of mind. And that which we do in a loving state of mind can become love made visible through our work.

The word *vocation* comes from the Latin root "to call." Your vocation then is a calling, and in a very deep sense finding your vocation can be finding yourself. When you have found your calling, you can give love through your work. In fact, love may be the key to success in mastering your vocation. It directs you to the special talents you can give to the world and shows you how to share them with others.

SIR JOHN MARKS TEMPLETON
NASSAU, BAHAMAS
JUNE 2000

Introduction

I n *The Living Workplace*, I explore the impact of the realities of the future workplace on the human soul and spirit. The search for spirituality is emerging as a growing force—hardly surprising in this climate of change and chaos. It is my conviction that as the 21st century unfolds, the workplace—and workers—will demand that this hunger for spirituality be satisfied, and will insist on a new language and a new approach to workplace relationships. It is also my conviction that few corporations are prepared to accept or understand the legitimacy or extent of this hunger and that they are, as a consequence, ill-prepared to make the radical shifts that will be demanded of them.

My hope is that *The Living Workplace* will inspire people to be visionaries in both their personal and professional lives; that it will encourage them to understand and come to terms with the intense and overwhelming spiritual longing that is gathering strength and power in them and among them. I hope that in this book, somewhere between the lines, they will sense new directions and from that foundation develop options that will help them come to grips with the extraordinary shifts already under way.

The Living Workplace is about creating change. If the book helps you change your life, if it gives you courage, if it inspires you to explore your life, then it will have been of value.

ANN COOMBS
SPRING 2001

> "Imagination
> is more important
> than knowledge."
>
> *Albert Einstein*

CHAPTER 1

Future Zone

F ierce competition for talent. A bidding war for a shrinking pool of knowledge workers. Virtual assistants. Greed. Cynicism. Commitment. Responsibility. Accountability. Living one's values. These will be the hallmarks of the highly competitive, challenging environment of the living workplace of the 21st century. Within a decade, the workplace will be dramatically different from the workplace of the century just ended.

What will be the realities of the future workplace? How will these realities affect workers and employers and how they perceive, understand and undertake the role of work? Who will define success? How will it be measured? Who will succeed, and who will not?

The Way We Were

In the 1950s and 1960s, employers asked workers to bring their hands to work. "Do your work. Follow orders. Don't rock the boat." That was the recipe for success.

In the 1970s and 1980s, employers asked workers to bring their brains to work. "Use your mind in ways that bring value to the company." That was the recipe for success.

In the 1990s, employers upped the ante. "Bring your hearts to work," they said. "We want you—in fact, we require you—to be really passionate about what you do."

As the decade, and the century, drew to a close, a few employers began to ask for even more: "Bring your soul to work," they said. "Bring your values and beliefs. Bring those things that have the deepest meaning for you."

And what did workers get in return? For most, it was a living wage and job security. For some, it was great satisfaction, advancement up the corporate ladder and applause from their peers. For a few, it yielded extraordinary wealth and recognition.

But as the 1980s gave way to the 1990s and then the 1990s drew to a close, workers found themselves in an increasingly high-pressure scramble to keep the job and the pension intact in times of continual reorganizing, reengineering and reforming; to keep a toehold on employment in times of slavish devotion to increasing shareholder value at any cost; to maintain some self-respect in the face of a prevailing attitude toward the worker as a dispensable part of the organization.

The 20th-century workplace upheaval, characterized by increasing disrespect, dis-ease and disharmony, continues as we move into the 21st century. But already the signs of the coming transformation are evident. Within a decade, the workplace balance will be irrevocably changed, the balance of power shifted.

The Way We Are

As the 21st century opens, employers continue to say at every opportunity that their greatest resource is the people who work for them. They speak sincerely about "empowering" employees, "respecting them" as human beings and helping them "fulfill their potential."

Indeed, many employers, especially large corporations, provide substantial benefit packages and other tangible and intangible tokens of their regard—company incentive trips, fitness facilities, employee-of-the-month awards, holiday parties, paid leave for volunteer work, employee share ownership plans and health benefits extended to same-sex partners (see the table below). All are designed to demonstrate that employees are valued. But they are also carefully calibrated to ensure a positive impact on the bottom line—a reality not lost on employees.

Benefits Wanted

What employees said they would like to have most	How various flexible benefits ranked among those that have them
1. Flexible benefit program: 34%	1. Elder care
2. Cash bonus geared to individual performance: 24%	2. Working from home
	3. Job sharing
3. Self-directed pension plan: 16%	4. Flex-time
4. Pension plan based on years of service: 15%	5. Paid time off
	6. Child care
5. Stock purchase plan: 6%	7. Discount programs
6. Cash bonus geared to group performance: 5%	

Source: "What the Boss Needs to Know,"
by Patricia Chisholm, *Maclean's*, May 29, 2000, page 20.

At the same time, corporations do not hesitate to cut, stop, move around, reorganize, change, refocus and outsource without regard for the devastating consequences of these continuing upheavals on their employees' working conditions, morale or career prospects. In the United States alone, for example, despite nearly a decade of stunning economic growth, job layoffs jumped from about 100,000 in 1989 to nearly 700,000 in 1999.[1]

"Despite the rhetoric of people being 'our most valuable resource,' the Western orientation to a throwaway lifestyle is alive and well at work. Employees, left to fend for themselves, are becoming migrant workers in an environment that shuns the mere suggestion of permanence or longer term commitment. In a sense, we are all self-employed in today's economy," says Ian Rose, president of IBR Consulting Services Ltd. in Vancouver, British Columbia.

The underlying truth, for a majority of firms, is that employees are valued only insofar as the bottom line and the demands of shareholders permit or encourage.

It is hardly surprising, then, that employees, especially those with in-demand knowledge and skills and those who have been through the upheaval of the reengineering-and-merging frenzy of the 1990s, are less and less inclined to accept these payments and gestures as sufficient compensation for what they must give in return— absolute, unquestioning loyalty; total commitment; and increasing hours of work underscored by worry, stress and uncertainty.

As the Conference Board of Canada reported in a study done in late 1999, "Employee morale is generally low in organizations at a time when organizations need extraordinary performance from ordinary people."

Some employees are already looking at their priorities, judging what their value is to their employers, and thinking carefully about what matters most to their employers. Increasingly, what matters to these workers is their dignity and self-respect. More and more of them are beginning to understand that while the balance of power remains in the hands of employers, employees also have power—the power to take their talents, skills and knowledge elsewhere. And more importantly, they are realizing that there are places that offer better options. An excellent benefits package and ingratiating words will no longer be enough to hold on to them.

Kathy Kane of K2Work/Life Solutions in Chicago agrees that evolving beliefs and behaviors are changing the way individuals view the corporation. "Employees feel more empowered to manage and maintain responsibility for their own employment, their own lives, their own well-being. Blind loyalty exists no longer; mutual respect, loyalty and commitment are the new expectations and behaviors."

"The concept of reciprocity in relationships is not new," says Christopher B. Galvin, chairman and chief executive officer of Motorola Inc. "The analogy in organizational life has been to parent–child: company provides, employee behaves. The new model is of marriage of equals: both require, both contribute. The spirit will change more than the form. Trust will become the key variable, and those who responsibly trust the most will win."

The Way We Will Be

The transformation is already in progress. The old business model of "employer tell–employee do" is changing, albeit more slowly in some organizations than others. The pace of change will continue to accelerate, however. Within a decade, the traditional workplace will evolve into one that will defy rigidity. The balance of power will be permanently altered.

The trend is already apparent. As *The Economist* reported, the patterns of working life are changing. "More frequent job changes, more freelancing, more working at home, more opportunity but also more uncertainty. The old social contract between employers and workers is being shredded." Just take a look at your human resources database for the past five years. Note the number of changes during that period. How many employees who were with the corporation five years ago are still there today?

How will it play out? One of the most obvious symbols, and greatest challenges, for employers during the next decade will be dealing with the war for talent. The initial challenge will be obtaining and retaining this new breed—employees who have expanded knowledge and skills, but who are also no longer willing to accept whatever employers tell them is necessarily valid and no longer willing to assume that whatever employers ask of employees is necessarily appropriate or in synch with their personal goals.

Many employers are already mystified. Why, with superb benefits, flexible working hours, top-level salaries and a pick of projects, do their key staff get restless?

Timothy Butler and James Waldroop attribute it to a search for happiness. "Many talented professionals leave their organizations because senior managers do not understand the psychology of work satisfaction; they assume that people who excel at their work are necessarily happy in their jobs. Sounds logical, but will [people] stay? The answer is, only if the job matches their deeply embedded life interests. [These] are long-held, emotionally driven passions, intricately entwined with personality and thus born of an indeterminate mix of nature and nurture. Deeply embedded life interests do not determine what people are good at—they drive what kinds of activities make them happy. At work, that happiness often translates into commitment. It keeps people engaged, and it keeps them from quitting."[2]

Restlessness and dissatisfaction are employee reactions to the unrelenting demand to remain current and competitive, and to the frenetic pace in every aspect of life. Changing jobs seems a temptingly simple way to get away from the pressure and into something that will bring greater happiness. This restlessness, however, can be dealt with only by changing fundamentals. A living workplace does this by responding to the quality of life, spirit and soul.

Employers will be also be faced with two other drivers—a shrinking labor force as the baby boomers reach retirement age, and raids by dot.com companies on that shrinking talent pool. Together, these factors will have a powerful impact—they will leave employers and human resources specialists reeling.

Today's workers absorbed the essence of the new corporate work-place either directly, by experiencing it, or indirectly, by watching their parents. They understand that individuals can no longer rely on corporations to take care of them. Nor can they count on labor unions, which are no longer as powerful as they were in the 1960s and 1970s. There is no such thing anymore as guaranteed, long-term employment. Employees *must* take responsibility for themselves.

And so workers are gradually beginning to think in terms of *career security* rather than *job security*. As frightening as this prospect may be, it is also liberating. It empowers workers to look on the employment contract as temporary not only because employers have been treating it that way, but also because employees now see the advantages to themselves. Increasingly, they are saying, "Yes, I will give you my knowledge, skills and time, but only for so long as it suits me. My commitment to you is good only for as long as you uphold your part of the working relationship or until something better comes along. And by the way, I am on the lookout all the time, even if it's not obvious."

Skill-Set Blues

Some employees, such as the highly sought-after technology work-ers, have already acted on the new view. They have had the advan-tage of esoteric knowledge and skills employers needed right now, at any price. As e-commerce expands and convergence continues, these individuals continue to wield their power.

But they are only the beginning. The cracks in the dam are show-ing. Soon the floodgates will open, and no sector will be left untouched.

Health care workers are already walking in the footsteps of soft-ware engineers and e-commerce Web designers. Pharmacists, for example, are desperately needed; there simply are not enough of them to go around. In 1999, in Canada alone, there were about 800 positions unfilled. In the United States, there were some 4,500 jobs open with no candidates in sight. Nurses, x-ray technicians, home care workers, orthopedic surgeons, oncologists, obstetricians . . . the list of supply shortages is long and growing.

The skilled trades too are crying the blues. Where are all the plumbers, carpenters, electricians and air-conditioning technicians we need to keep our day-to-day world in good order?

The biggest crisis in the making is in the service sector. Corporations have discovered that it is a lot easier to *promise* good service than it is to *deliver* it, because good service involves every level of the company and virtually all workers, many of whom do not currently see themselves as part of the service sector.

Often dismissed as the minimum-wage McJob and disposable staff zone, the service sector is a critical one that includes managers, professionals, technicians, salespeople, administrative assistants and transportation workers, as well as many other white- and blue-collar workers. In fact, the service sector already accounts for 80 percent of employment in the United States.[3]

In the good old days, coffee pourers, hamburger flippers and sales-clerks were a dime a dozen—and treated that way. But the good old days are vanishing as the labor pool, and especially the number of younger workers, shrinks. Macy's flagship department store in New York City, for example, is holding job fairs and offering substantial signing bonuses in order to recruit sales staff.[4]

Retailers, who have long relied on casual and part-time workers, are particularly feeling the service worker pinch—and taking a direct hit on the bottom line. As *The Globe and Mail* reported on March 28, 2000, a Retail Council of Canada study revealed that retail employee turnover increased by 50 percent in the previous two years. Moreover, retailers experienced record levels of losses from internal theft, fraud and errors. The average amount stolen by employees doubled in the same period. A consultant who worked on the study called the results a wake-up call for retailers to develop programs that give employees incentives to stay and that foster employee loyalty.

The reality just now being driven home to retailers is entirely predictable. In a sector noted for inefficiency, poor service, negligible staff training, frequent "out-of-stock" notices, few weekend deliveries and policies that do not meet consumers' expectations or needs, both employees and customers have been frustrated.

Recently, I made a trip to a specialty garden store to buy a birthday gift for my cousin, but I wanted to be sure the gift could be returned. The answer? No refund. Exchange only. *And by the way, you will be charged a 15-percent restocking fee.* Since I was paying full retail price and had not had individual service, I was astounded by the answer.

Clearly, the focus of the entire service sector will have to change. As customers continue to demand more for less, as the pressure to staff call centers and help desks increases, the careless "there are lots more where you came from" attitude will be forced to change. But that change must first be signalled by the management. By respecting and valuing the workers who keep the day-to-day business spinning, giving them the training and support they need, and remunerating them at levels sufficient to provide a decent quality of life, management creates an environment of care.

The Labor Whirlpool

The balance of power between employers and employees is shifting for several reasons, one of which is high demand for workers to fill jobs created by a booming economy. According to the U.S. Department of Labor, for example, unemployment in that country is at a 30-year low.[5]

But there are other factors at work—factors that will ease the pressure for a period of time. One, there is still strong support for the traditional, hierarchical business model. Although the support may be tentatively expressed, the traditional model is still regarded by many as the model of choice. After all, authoritarian, centralized power structures have yielded results that still speak with a strong voice. "We have done this for many years and it works. We are very profitable. Why should we change?" is the argument advanced by those who refuse to see or are unable to see or innately fear to see the transformation in progress. Many of them hold the reins of power in terms of control of capital, and they will use their current strategies to protect their wealth, status and authority.

Two, these traditionalists will be aided by an anomaly in the labor pool. The baby boomers are nearing the generally accepted retirement age of 65, but as a group they are not necessarily ready to step out of the workforce. They are already finding ways to remain active in the business world. Some are successfully challenging the 65-and-retire rule and hanging on to their jobs. Others are stepping into contract work or reinventing themselves as virtual assistants or entrepreneurs.

And three, there are new sources of employees. Some corporations are looking for (and finding) workers among those previously classified as less able or less desirable—for example, the physically disabled or mentally challenged. Some have lowered the educational standard demanded for certain kinds of jobs, thus enlarging the pool of prospects. As well, North America still remains the continent of choice for workers from many different parts of the world. Thanks to technology, some can participate without immigrating, but many well-educated, highly skilled workers are making their way to Canada and the United States.

The inevitable outcome will be increased competition among these older, reluctant-to-retire workers, younger workers just beginning their careers, and immigrants and off-shore workers. The resulting struggle may well force down wages in some job categories, and possibly affect the scale and variety of benefits employers feel the need to offer.

It will not be all that easy, however, even for employers able to take advantage of this competition. They will still have to cope with the challenges of integrating a mixed workforce. What will happen when a seasoned, experienced 65-year-old worker, who is needed based on his or her knowledge, is assigned to work with a 30-year-old with an entirely different life view? Add to this the complexities in understanding and accepting workers from different cultures, of different races, and with different values and expectations. The facets of the transformation will be complex indeed.

One might expect that young companies founded by young entre-preneurs with fresh perspectives and a clean slate will have an advantage. But they will be facing the same pressures as well-established corporations. In fact, they may be at a disadvantage. For them, the search for talent will be just as fierce and possibly even more demanding because they will be challenged financially to meet the demands for benefits and incentives. They too will eventually have to turn to older workers and newcomers from other cultures. Will they be any more successful at assimilating and accommodat-ing a diverse workforce?

The Technology Revolution

Technology has already been a breathtakingly forceful agent of change. "The key design element in the new economy is time", says Thornton May, vice-president of research at Cambridge Technology Partners and an adjunct faculty member at the John E. Anderson Graduate School of Management at UCLA. "Today, under pressure of accelerating change, the past and future have been fused into a single tense: the present. The present is real time and real time is the only time."

As well as compressing time and speeding up the pace of work, technology has changed beyond recognition the ways in which work is done and business is conducted. Perhaps the most obvious and profound effect has been the technological revolution's spawning of many new kinds of work for new kinds of workers—those who design, manufacture, install, adapt and operate the tech tools on which we have come to depend.

At the same time, it has eliminated or reshaped many administra-tive, manufacturing and service jobs. Receptionists have been replaced by voice-mail, auto workers work with robots, dairy farmers use sophisticated software to track milk production and feed costs, and real estate agents show "virtual" properties. Businesses contract with programmers half a world away, and writers deliver copy by e-mail. Companies pay employees by direct deposit. Manufacturers integrate their systems with those of their customers, track customers' inventory and ship automatically as stock levels are depleted.

Christine Durst and Michael Haaren, president and chief operating officer, respectively, of Staffcentrix, LLC, predict that technology will make "virtual" workers a critical component in the future workplace. "The majority of workers will no longer commute," says Durst. "The workforce will divide into the 'theres' (those who have to be 'there') and the 'there nots' (virtual workers who do not need to be 'there')." Haaren adds, "I also see a split between those who can 'swim' in technology and those who cannot. The non-tech population will be much larger—and much poorer—than the tech group."

Whether "there" or "not there," everyone is already expected to be available 24 hours a day, 7 days a week, because the means to do so exist. Soon, for example, the New York Stock Exchange will be open for business around the clock. Thus technology has become a tyrant as well as an enabler, a barrier as well as a connector.

Technology in the form of pagers, laptops, cell phones and other electronic devices allows workers to take the office to wherever is most convenient. The flip side is the danger that the workday will literally never end. Because the virtual office does not depend on time of day, physical space or geographical location, the accepted norm may easily become one of working all day, every day.

"The key to technological effectiveness is the behavior of the people using it," says Steven Zeisler, founder and director of Zeisler Associates, Inc. in Hockessin, Delaware. "We all need to learn how to use tools to their fullest capability, rather than as a mere augmentation—or worse—of a former technology. It always amazes me how people have turned so much good technology into impediments. Cell phones and voice-mail have become time traps, pagers and beepers going off everywhere at any time, interrupting idea time and spontaneous interactions. E-mail becomes a way for managers to avoid face-to-face conversations with people."

What has not changed and *will not* change, however, is the need for specialization, for brains, for ideas, for creativity, for innovation. The definition of *knowledge worker* will be broadened to include not only those who have specific, sought-after technical skills, but also those who have the education, imagination, intellectual capacity and communication skills to deal with an increasingly competitive, diverse and global marketplace.

At the same time, technology has provided an escape hatch for workers eager to change their terms of employment and determined to assert more control over their lives. Because it is possible to work at a distance and because it is now possible to find work anywhere in the world without leaving home, self-employment has become a much more viable and attractive option. Indeed, in North America SOHO (small office/single owner, home office) workers are growing at a rate significantly faster than the total workforce.

Not long ago, many corporations were leery of consultants, especially the SOHO breed. They looked on these entrepreneurs as the unemployable or employees-in-waiting. When I opened my business in 1980, for example, it was a challenge at first to persuade prospective clients to take me seriously as a consulting professional capable of providing value in an array of industry sectors. At the time, women who operated businesses from home-based offices were usually dismissed as "just freelancers" or small-time craft makers.

Today, the picture is markedly different. Staffcentrix's Haaren says he considers virtual assistants, what he terms "neoSOHOs," as invaluable growth partners. His view is that businesses of every size can benefit from the many skills that virtual assistants bring to the workplace. Durst adds, "Statistics also show that virtual office workers are 10 percent to 20 percent more productive than permanent office workers, yielding significant savings and increased productivity."

Christopher Galvin of Motorola Inc. agrees with Haaren and Durst. "Virtual organizations with smart minds in different geographies and time zones will have the winning model—not those that accumulate resources under their own roofs," he says.

Some corporate managers continue to cling to a prejudiced view of smaller-scale entrepreneurs and self-employed professionals, but many are changing their position. Having pared their workforces to a minimum, sometimes even below minimum, corporations are now finding themselves short of talent at crucial junctures. SOHOs are suddenly attractive: available on short notice, around only as long as needed, and paid by the job. They bring specific, valuable skills and knowledge gained from dealing with a diverse client base, as well as commitment without any expensive human resources issues such as depression and stress, both of which are increasing in the workplace.

For workers who have been pushed out of employment, who are increasingly uncomfortable in corporate environments where they do not feel valued, or who have a high need for independence, technology provides the tools they need to make a living on custom-made terms. For these workers, quality of life is so compelling that they are willing to give up the benefits packages, the incentives, and the comforts and allures of a regular job and steady paycheck.

As more and more workers begin to question the value of loyalty and commitment to organizations that do not seem to value them, they too will exercise the entrepreneurial option. And employers will be forced to adjust and adapt both by relying on them to an increasing extent and by changing the way they deal with the staff they still have and desperately need to retain. And that will accentuate another fact of life with which they will be required to deal—the growth of greed.

Greed and Cynicism

Greed is as alive and well in today's world of commerce as it has been for generations. The question is, does it have a greater impact today than before? The answer is yes. One only needs to look at the merger-and-acquisition mania of the 1990s and the huge bonuses paid to already extremely well-rewarded chief executives.

Will greed continue to grow and influence how business works and how the workplace operates? Again the answer is yes. Look at the millions paid for dot.com stocks long before they had actually produced anything and, indeed, without any serious expectation that they ever would.

No one would argue with the need for a corporation to make a profit. Clearly, it must if it is to survive; otherwise, everyone loses. But if the quest for profit is done without caring and compassion, without recognition of the value of employees, without just reward to employees for their contributions, and with a focus on profit-taking and obeisance to shareholders, that is greed.

If a corporation operates by the creed of greed, its workers will be negatively affected, even if only at a subconscious level. If the managerial mind-set is to make a profit at any cost, it will eventually change the way people within the corporation deal with one another. Trust, loyalty and commitment will be damaged because all employees will know that they count for nothing if they get in the way of fiscal advantage for those in positions of power.

No one should be surprised that greed breeds cynicism in the workforce. As workers struggle to pay their mortgages and worry about keeping their jobs, they see merger consultants walk away with millions in consulting fees and the corporation's directors and senior managers rewarded with astonishingly valuable stock options and other payments.

Who can blame them for reacting with cynicism when they hear the CEO tell them once again how important they are to the corporation, but "We regret we are unable to provide raises because . . ." or "We will have to do more with less as a team because . . ."? Canadian Airlines is a classic example. In 1999, after years of employees watching staff being pared, forgoing raises, investing sweat equity and making many other sacrifices, the corporation was summarily folded into Air Canada. Canadian's employees were not given any solid guarantees that once the dust settled their contributions or their loyalty would be repaid.

Nor should anyone be surprised as the next generation enters the workforce with greed and cynicism as part of their psychological makeup. After all, they have watched and listened to their predecessors express their frustrations, worry about job security, suffer the consequences of mergers and reorganizations, and see their trust, loyalty and commitment repaid with callous disregard for the value of their services and contributions.

The new generation has also witnessed the dizzying financial success of those fortunate few knowledge workers with esoteric skills that happened to be the commodity most needed, highly prized and lavishly rewarded as the technological revolution took hold. Why should *they* settle for less? And why should *they* wait and worry and wonder the way their parents did? Their attitude is "I want it now. I'm not prepared to wait."

Lawrence Pentland, president of Dell Computer Corporation in Toronto, is one of many corporate leaders concerned with the challenge of recruiting and retaining employees. His company is pursuing an innovative benefits plan to attract and keep the people it needs.

"I see the cost of attracting top talent into the organization having a tremendous impact on the future of business," says Randy Bartsch, president and CEO of British Columbia's Magnatex, Inc. "In the same way the power shifted from the movie studios to the acting talent, the same has happened in sport, where the top talent commands a huge quantum over simply the good players. I believe this same trend will manifest itself in business. The amount of money required to attract and keep the best talent in your industry will make it difficult for small market players to compete. The smaller players will have to find new ways to adapt, establish niches and reinvent themselves and their roles in the future of business."

As the war for talent heats up and the bidding intensifies, the result will be that only the richest and largest of corporations will survive, because they will be able to pay enough to get the best workers to ensure their core interests are served. The rest will outsource to what futurist Joseph F. Coates, president of Coates & Jarratt, Inc., of Washington, D.C., calls the "contingent workforce"—temporary help drawn from local and offshore contract workers and consultants with specific skills needed for specific tasks. The middle-level companies, finding themselves increasingly unable to lure and keep the workers they need, will be absorbed by the giants or go out of business altogether. Unless, of course, they are wise enough to understand that, greed and cynicism apart, workers are human beings who still willingly give their trust, loyalty and commitment to employers who offer trust, loyalty and commitment in return.

Success, Survival and Soul

The corporations that will survive and thrive, irrespective of size, are those that understand something else—how success is understood and measured.

There are, and always have been, different understandings and measures of what constitutes success, including money, social status, public praise, the approval of peers, the satisfaction inherent in doing one's best, and feelings of self-worth stemming from a belief that one's work is of value to society. All these measures will continue to be accepted. But as the transformation of the workplace takes hold and as more and more people ask themselves what really, truly matters to them, another measure, just now beginning to emerge, will become increasingly important.

Consider the Five O'Clock Club, a self-described employee advocacy organization with 20 branches across the United States. As of 1999, according to *The Economist*, most of its members were 35 to 55 years old. A third of them were earning more than $100,000 a year. By any economic measure, these people are highly successful. Yet they do not see themselves that way. All are questioning their goals, values and needs. One member, an Internet manager who had made $3 million in the previous 18 months, "still feels left behind." Obviously, money and the material trappings it can buy are no longer sufficient to satisfy these people's inner yearnings.

And for what do they yearn? Stability. Security. Quality of life. The opportunity to turn their dreams, whatever those dreams may be, into reality. To come home from work each day with soul, spirit and values intact.

We often hear the terms soul and spirit used interchangeably, as though the two refer to one and the same thing. In fact, philosophers, religious scholars and metaphysicists have long debated the meaning and scope of soul and spirit, with some ultimately integrating the concepts into a single notion and others seeing a clear distinction between the two. I hold with the latter. Soul, I believe, is that non-physical part of a person in which resides his or her intellectual and emotional core. Spirit is the vital essence imbuing that core. Spirit expresses itself within us in many energizing ways. It is continually changing, but always remains connected to our entire immaterial consciousness. Soul is the essential completeness of who we are: the sum total of our spirit as it changes and moves within us. No question, soul and spirit are inextricably linked, but seeing them in light of their differences enhances our understanding of what they—and we—are.

As the 20th century drew to a close, employees were already showing reluctance to leave their real selves—their souls and spirits—at home. They are no longer willing to bring only part of themselves to work or even assume different personalities to suit their employers' preferences. They want to be their whole selves all day, and they consider a working environment that encourages personal authenticity as important as challenging work, interesting assignments and good salaries.

Astute employers have already recognized the nature of the change now evolving and have opted to accommodate themselves to it. But for what purpose? To make their employees feel better? More than likely, the motive is to ensure against a negative impact on the bottom line, although this is rarely stated. "If we do not ask you to bring your soul to work, you will not be fully engaged on behalf of the corporation and you will not be as productive as we want or need you to be."

This is valid as far as it goes, but will it succeed? Will it help employers win the war for talent? Will it improve productivity, help them retain choice employees, enhance the bottom line and improve shareholder value? Yes, if it is done consciously and with conscience.

Senior managers and executives must be able to see and deal with employees as people. When that day comes—when the CEO sees the souls within as well as the faces without—the company will be telling the truth when it says its greatest asset is its people. The company will also be well on the way to putting living soul into the workplace.

Wise and courageous CEOs and the visionaries among senior managers will succeed in putting the soul into the workplace because they will truly understand that this is not a matter of core competencies or best practices. They will succeed because they truly understand human behavior, maintain a position of overall corporate well-being, and balance the integrity of employees with the need to make the profit that keeps the company alive and well. When such leaders ask their employees to bring their total values to work, workers will bring them willingly, knowing that their values are integrated with the mission of the corporation.

By demonstrating every day in every way that the corporation is a place where important work is done and people's lives and dreams can be realized, these enlightened organizations will protect and enhance the life of the corporation and its economic value. They will survive and they will thrive because they understand and live the concept of soul.

Enlightened Accountability

Will working for an enlightened corporation erase fear, stress and confusion from employees' lives? Will it mean a life of peace and plenty? No, not entirely. The world of commerce will continue to be a volatile, demanding, often chaotic environment.

Will it erase the greed factor? Will employees magically turn into uncomplaining, loyal and committed workers who live heart-and-soul for the company? No, not entirely, given human nature.

But enlightened corporations will attract and hold those for whom honor, trust and truth are at least as important as salary scales and prospects for advancement. They will appeal to employees who define themselves less and less by what they do and more and more by who they are.

By the same token, employees must still understand that they have entered a relationship. They must give what they have promised to give. They must deal honestly and fairly with their colleagues and employers. They must expect to be held accountable for the quality of their work and for their actions, which affect everyone else in the company. They must be as supportive, encouraging and reliable as they expect their employers to be. And they must expect to pay the price if they fail to give as they receive.

The Values Zone

The 21st century workplace is crystallizing into the new, emerging forms. What will it look like?

The writing is already on the wall. During the past 10 years, the "look and feel" of both blue- and white-collar jobs changed dramatically. Within another 10 years, the nature of employment will be further changed to the extent that it will be virtually unrecognizable when compared with what we see today.

Art Shostak, professor of Sociology at Drexel University in Philadelphia, forecasts a dramatic change in the quality of jobs. When I interviewed him in July 1999, he said, "Technology will exacerbate the strain on work and workers. Many workers are likely to find their work increasingly dumbed-down, while a few will find their work migraine-inviting in its ceaseless complexity."

In a recent conversation with Vancouver-based futurist Frank Ogden, we discussed the topic of the changing workplace. His view is that jobs as such will disappear. But he added, "There will be more work to be done than ever before. There will also be more opportunity than ever before. The workplace won't be a fixed place. Task forces will be called together to accomplish whatever the current project is and disband when it is finished."

Ogden and I agree that those who will survive and thrive are the self-employed. I am convinced as well that those who receive a different kind of education are also likely to succeed. Regrettably, few North American educational institutions are creating alternatives to the traditional approach to education. I find this perplexing because the necessity seems so obvious. Given the way in which the workplace is evolving, it seems logical to assume that the educational system should evolve as well.

Unlike Ogden, I believe jobs as such will still be available. But I also believe there will be fewer of them and that they will be offered primarily by mega-corporations, which will dominate the marketplace. Employees will be expected to work in units or teams that form, dissolve and re-form as required. They will be supplemented by consultants, contract staff and external project teams drawn from the expanding e-lance economy. Many of these independent visionaries will begin their working careers as employees and then choose the entrepreneurial option. Others will go straight from the classroom to the frontline as a SOHO or micro-entrepreneur.

There will be a huge increase in the number of entrepreneurs, micro-enterprises and e-lancers. They will get the bulk of their business from the mega-corporations in the form of short-term contracts or projects. Project management will become the byword. For the e-lancers, the global opportunities will be unlimited.

And who will survive and who will thrive in this competitive and values-driven environment?

Alan Keith, vice-president and chief administrative officer of Lucas Digital Ltd. LLC, points to creativity and culture as critical factors in retaining good people. His company provides superior employee benefits, workplace opportunities for personal growth and development, and a familial spirit. But Keith recognizes that Lucas Digital has a big advantage over companies operating in more traditional sectors. "We would not be as successful as we are in retaining talent if it were not for the opportunities to work on the coolest and most leading-edge work in our field." Having said that, he adds, "Our challenge will come in how we create this same type of winning culture and teamwork in a more fragmented environment."

"The ones who survive and thrive are those who are smart and courageous enough to realize the business value of what I call the three Ms of human asset management—measuring, managing and maximizing their human asset base," says Richard A. Lippin, M.D., president of The Lippin Group and founding president of the International Arts-Medicine Association. "Those who do not understand and leverage that asset are doomed to extinction."

The ascendant mega-corporations will have a clear sense of core values, be genuinely committed to those values, and communicate those values clearly, effectively and consistently to their employees. They will be committed to such values as truth, caring, compassion and fairness. They will remain true to those values even as they adapt their business strategies and practices to respond to market-driven changes. Their employees will be attracted and retained by the promise and the reality of an ethical workplace.

The employees who make it will be those who share the mega-corporations' core values, who bring their creativity and initiative as well as their commitment and skills to work, and who develop the talents of their co-workers as eagerly as they seek to develop their own.

The entrepreneurs who make it will be those who demonstrate truth, honor and commitment as clearly and compellingly as they show initiative, creativity and service.

Soul, spirit and values. In words. In actions. These guiding principles will drive the transformation. Those who strive for moral strength and economic well-being will be the leaders.

The others will be left behind.

"Truth is truth to the
end of reckoning."

William Shakespeare,
Measure for Measure,
Act V

CHAPTER 2

Truth & Consequences

In *The Doctrine of Men,* Confucius wrote, "Absolute truth is indestructible. Being indestructible, it is eternal."

For me, there is no shade of gray about truth. As Leo Tolstoy observed in *War and Peace,* "For us, with the rule of right and wrong given us by Christ, there is nothing for which we have no standard."

Truth has many dimensions. In my view, it has an intrinsic importance and value that affects every part of our lives, whether we recognize it or not. We need to speak, act and be consistent with the truth at all times. Otherwise, we enter a wasteland where the absence of truth damages our souls. I also believe that truth*less*ness is endemic in today's workplace.

How is truth defined in today's workplace? How is truth related to ethics? How do we understand ethics and ethical standards? How do we express them in workplace behaviors? What happens when our personal values and standards—our concept of truth and how it should be expressed—are at variance with what we find in the workplace?

Defining Truth

Is truth a firm, steady beacon we all understand and accept? Or is it flexible and dependent on one's personal view?

Dr. Michael Pountney, associate priest at St. Paul's Church in Toronto, is of the view that in the pre-modern world there was one truth for all. The concept of universal truth, as shown in the section below, was well understood and embraced as an ideal by humankind. Although the tenets of each religious faith were expressed differently, such tenets stood, and still stand, on this foundation. All people generally translated universal truth into commonly accepted values—such as honesty, kindness, charity, love, honor, justice and compassion—to guide daily life.

Truth for All

The concept of universal truth, or eternal verities, has been shared across time, space, religion and culture by all humankind. Universal truth may be simply stated as two fundamental principles:

1. There is only one God.
2. Treat others as you wish to be treated.

Today, Dr. Pountney says, the concept of a truth for all has given way to what he calls "truth for the moment." While it is unbending, it is also flexible and individual. Although it may reflect long-accepted values, such as honesty, kindness and honor, it may not be firmly rooted in them. It is the individual's truth because it fits the needs of the moment. But a moment from now it may change and still be called truth. It is regarded as truth because it is based on the individual's perceptions of what is right and appropriate at that moment, in those circumstances, for that situation.

Is defining truth as "of the moment" necessarily wrong? No, of course not. As the *Talmud* so eloquently and succinctly expresses it, "We do not see things as they are, we see things as we are." A modern writer, David Lyle Jeffrey, professor emeritus of English Literature at the University of Ottawa, puts it this way: "The recognition of truth depends in part upon the authenticity of one's intention to find truth."

Although there are certainly exceptions, most of us would not presume that our truth is the one and only truth that must be accepted and lived exactly as we would prescribe. Certainly, in today's diverse workplace, acceptance and tolerance of different faiths and cultures are necessary ingredients for living in the harmony that supports honesty, kindness, honor and truth.

Corporate Truth

What is truth for the corporation? The organization is, after all, the construct of many individuals. How is truth determined for this collective entity? Who decides? Is it the truth because the corporation's mission statement says it is? Is it the truth because independent facts support the declaration? Is it a guiding principle visibly applied, or is it a flexible commodity used to persuade, manipulate or even deceive for immediate gain or some other compelling purpose?

For the growing number of individual workers who seek a workplace of integrity, these are not idle questions. Such employees crave a spiritually supportive workplace. They need and want a workplace of integrity. They want a workplace where truth is defined in a way they can accept. They want a constant truth that connects operations, expectations and practices from one day to the next. Workers are gradually beginning to reject truth*less*ness. They are becoming less willing to accept flexibility in corporate practices that have no principled foundation.

All corporations, as a matter of course, present themselves as entities of integrity engaged honorably in the pursuit of economic gain. Their mission statements, vision statements, workplace standards, human resources policies and business practices are framed in the language of fairness, respect and honor. Their leaders are generally well-intentioned, principled people who believe what they are saying. Their difficulty, however, is how to maintain these standards in the face of a challenging, competitive marketplace. The temptation to jettison something that has become inconvenient or damaging to the bottom line, even if only temporarily, is always present and highly seductive.

Unfortunately, many corporate leaders are so pressed by internal and external demands and expectations that they constantly redefine truth. Yesterday's truth? Well, that was yesterday. Today is different, tomorrow will be different again. Besides, what was yesterday's truth anyway? Who could possibly be expected to remember in the rush of events and the crushing pressure to adapt and cope?

The Parameters of Truth

For workers, discovering, discerning and living their truth in the workplace is equally challenging. They must know what their personal truth is, they must decide whether yesterday's corporate truth is still the truth today, and they must decide what they can accept and what they cannot. This takes extraordinary courage because they too are pressed by internal and external demands, expectations and responsibilities. Challenging an employer is an act that rarely comes without serious consequences, especially if that challenge questions what is presented as truth.

In today's corporate world, there are regrettably few examples of corporations of honor, integrity and authenticity that acknowledge and operate consistently within parameters of a steady truth. One needs only to listen to announcements from head office or track media campaigns. The messages are often contradictory. For workers, the result is confusion and distrust. As they find the ground beneath them constantly shifting, they feel themselves sinking in a quagmire of internal conflict.

Employees also find themselves nudged toward distrust and cynicism when they see corporate leaders behaving in dishonest or dishonorable ways, for example, by spending company funds to entertain unnecessarily or providing company contracts to personal contacts who are not always the most qualified.

The Spiritually Sustaining Workplace

The spiritually aware corporation is one that creates a trusting, respectful and truth-filled environment. It has a clear sense of its own values, communicates those values clearly, incorporates those values into its words and actions, and encourages employees to do the same. It ensures that the values are expressions of integrity and honor and also that they underscore, relate to and support everything the company does. There are no exceptions. It must apply to all dealings with employees, customers, suppliers, allies, shareholders and everyone else who has any contact or association with the corporation.

What are the characteristics of the spiritually sustaining workplace? How can one recognize it? How can one develop it? The core principles are honor, respect and the pursuit of excellence. These form the foundation on which a spiritually sustaining workplace can be built. To build on that foundation, a workplace needs a visionary leader with a degree of humility. I call this visionary leader a *servant* leader because he or she leads sensitively and effectively while listening to and acknowledging the needs and views of followers. The tables below—one listing the characteristics of a spiritually sustaining workplace, and the second providing a guide for the servant leader—address these fundamentals.

Recognizing Spirituality in the Workplace

A spiritually sustaining workplace has these characteristics:
- Honors the Creator who exists in all human beings.
- Respects and develops human potential.
- Pursues and supports excellence at every level.
- Shares profits.

Being a Servant Leader

The servant leader creates a spiritually sustaining workplace using these 10 steps as a framework or guide.

1. Determine how to support employees' discernment skills.
2. Create a survey on the importance of spirituality to employees.
3. Review the results with a view to bringing openness to the evolvement of spirituality in the workplace.
4. Be willing to place spirituality in the company's plan for cultural and other change.
5. Clearly define and acknowledge the true realities of the workplace, for example, by conducting a spiritual framework survey (addressed more fully in Chapter 7, The Spiritual Worker).
6. Develop an environment of trust, truth and respect.
7. Bring external advisors in to address employees about spiritual and other issues important to them.

8. Be a living example of honesty and integrity.
9. Support diversity among employees and their points of view.
10. Value and reward individual and team contributions.

Responsibility and Accountability

"Over the last month, I've witnessed a business owner tell a trumped-up but flimsy story in an attempt to wriggle out of paying an honest contractor's bill," writes Cynthia L. Kemper, president of Edgewalkers International, in *Edgewalkers Weekly Insight*.[6] "In another situation, I heard a man brag about lying to an employee so that he could avoid a difficult confrontation and save himself some time. Then there was a woman who was chastised unfairly by her boss because he was too weak to take responsibility for his own errors, choosing to blame her instead. These stories originate in the United States and Canada. But they happen everywhere."

In 1999, a survey by InfoCheck Ltd., a Canadian reference-checking company, found that more than one-third of job applicants, across every sector and at every level from general office help to senior executives, routinely falsified information on their resumes. This was a 9 percent increase over the findings of the firm's 1998 survey. Why? We can only speculate. Perhaps it indicates a fundamental change in what truth means to us. Perhaps corporations are perceived as being elastic with the truth—so why should we not be elastic too? Regardless of the reason, the effect is to corrode the relationship of trust that is essential for a truthful environment.

On the job, many employees routinely do personal photocopying at their employers' expense or walk away with office supplies for personal use or overstate claims for work-related expenses or use company time for personal business. Often the rationale is that "Everybody does it." Certainly, the odds of this type of behavior taking root are increased by the similar actions of colleagues, peers and managers. Over the long term, these small acts are just as destructive to the relationship of trust as is lying to get the job in the first place.

As workers seek spiritually supportive workplaces, they must face the reality that truth requires living a truthful life. They must bring truthful character, actions and integrity to the workplace, or they will contribute to a corrosion of atmosphere that will ultimately damage the very thing they seek.

To claim the right to a spiritually sustaining work environment, everyone—from the office cleaner to the CEO—has to look closely at what is going to sustain the spirit, and then act on the truth of that knowledge and awareness. Everyone has to be prepared to act in a responsible way and be accountable for workplace behaviors and actions. For example, if you, an employee, claim the right to a spiritually sustaining environment and if you see circumstances that you believe are unreasonable, unfair or untruthful, you must be prepared to act on that knowledge in the same way that you would act in your own private life. Otherwise, you are abrogating your responsibility and betraying the relationship of trust between you and your employer.

In a sense, employees must acquire a double vision. It comes from knowing about and balancing two sets of values—personal and corporate. This is not always easy, given that individuals of different faiths and cultures may hold different values. Their responsibility is to decide for themselves what values are most important for them as individuals, and whether their personal values and those of the corporation are sufficiently aligned.

Employees must also accept that their colleagues may not share some or all of their most deeply held personal values. They must decide for themselves whether they can live with that difference. It is neither fair nor reasonable to expect colleagues or employers to change their views or values. It is the responsibility of the individual to take appropriate action.

Intending Truth

Conducting oneself with honor, integrity and truth day-to-day is very difficult in a world that does not seem to emphasize those qualities consistently. There are so many times when human beings fall short of their own standards and intentions. But the effort must be there and it must be sustained for all our sakes.

In the workplace, consistent and accurate memory of the facts is as important as the truth itself. Denying, shaping or shading the truth, inadvertently or deliberately, can be destructive to the truthful environment.

At the same time, circumstances change, often very quickly. For sound strategic reasons it may be unwise or even impossible to explain the quick turnabout. What employees may perceive as misusing or denying the truth may be a necessary action or simply an inadvertent oversight in the hectic swirl of events and demands. In today's time-pressured corporate environment, we are often forced to develop our thoughts and strategies as we go along. In my experience, it is not that the CEO does not want to tell the truth or intends to withhold the truth. Often, it is just that he or she does not have time to fully assess all the consequences and the impact they will have on each facet of the organization.

Both the corporation's leaders and its employees owe each other the moral obligation of good faith. This means accepting that people mean to tell the truth and that compromises are sometimes necessary. Showing good faith and relevance will make a difference.

The line can be, and often is, a very fine one to walk. The question will always be whether it is possible or practical. The problem, of course, is that they can be accused of being sparse with the truth or of not revealing relevant facts. They also run the risk of falling victim to the rumor mill.

However, if employees are confident that for the most part they are told as much as can be told and that what they are told is the truth or sincerely thought to be the truth, they are much more likely to accept the occasional extenuating circumstance. And so they should, because, after all, managers are fallible human beings too. *Truth lies in the intent.*

Of course, the reverse is also true. Truth of intention must be balanced against lapses in judgment up the ranks as well as down. Occasional forgetfulness or thoughtlessness is one thing; making a habit of being very casual with the truth is another. Being casual with the truth is so simple to do and so easily rationalized. It is also an act often done and then denied.

The greatest damage to the trustful environment occurs when employers or employees are consistently perceived as consciously refusing or neglecting to tell the truth, of manipulating the truth or of using those parts of the truth that suit them in order to gain power at someone else's expense.

Loving Truth

"Love" is a word and an emotion generally shunned in the workplace. Overworked and overused, it is regarded as a feeling totally inappropriate for the practical, down-to-earth place that a business needs to be. And yet love is an essential component of truth and trust. As Pierre Teilhard de Chardin said in *The Phenomenon of Man,* "Love alone is capable of uniting living beings in such a way as to complete and fulfill them, for it alone takes them and joins them by what is deepest within themselves."

For the most part, love is distrusted in the workplace. Why? Perhaps it is the fear of becoming too close and therefore obligated. Perhaps it is the fear of being rejected or betrayed. Perhaps it is the fear of admitting dependence; being dependent is often equated with being powerless.

All of us have experienced the dichotomy of seeking the sustenance of affection and trust and yet at the same time resisting it. I recall, for example, being invited by a prominent international bank to deliver a presentation on the future. My instructions were clear: Make it very, very inspirational, but mention neither love nor hope.

Recently, I was at a meeting of high-ranking, successful women from a cross section of industries. When I asked them how many felt their working environments were supportive, the atmosphere became very uneasy, even a little tense. They were prepared to discuss the topic, and eventually all of them admitted in one way or another that they saw many opportunities for trust and truth to be brought to their workplaces. It was rare, however, for them to use the word *love* in any context.

And yet corporations want to inspire and motivate their employees. They want their employees to bring their full sense of purpose to work. How can employers succeed if they refuse to admit the existence and value of affection? How can they build trust without admitting need?

Suspect Truths

Sustaining an environment of truth and trust requires a great deal more than declaring it to be so and encouraging employees to live up to their spiritual quotient or emotional IQ. Are truth and trust, integrity and honor incorporated into the culture of the corporation? What is the evidence for it? What speaks against it? Is the concept of a spiritually sustaining workplace viewed as a useful marketing tool? Does the corporation use words such as spirit, soul, trust, integrity and truth simply as surface polish? Or are these concepts deeply rooted in the corporation's every word and deed?

Given the record of corporate actions in the 1980s and 1990s, declarations of spiritually supportive workplaces are more likely to be greeted with cynicism and suspicion than openhearted acceptance. Much as 21st-century workers hunger for the sustenance of trust and crave spiritually sustaining workplaces, they have ample reason to be wary.

After the ferocious downsizing, reengineering and merging of the closing years of the 20th century, it is difficult not to conclude that honor, trust and truth are convenient commodities for corporations to shape and use at will. Corporate leaders at the time spoke compellingly and sincerely about the absolute necessity for radical workforce cuts on the grounds that business imperatives in an increasingly competitive global economy demanded it. Workers who survived the firestorm were exhorted to be flexible, adaptable and committed. Turbulence, insecurity and fear were dismissed as inconveniences. They were viewed as minor prices to be paid in exchange for the greater goal.

Peer pressure, always a force to be reckoned with, was particularly intense during this period and at all levels within organizations. Few dared to speak against the wishes of their Boards of Directors. To do so would be to invite retribution. Even fewer dared to speak of conscience.

It is unlikely that the managers charged with the task of carrying out the orders did so with relish. It is extremely unlikely that they did it with intent to crush careers and destroy lives. But how real and how deep was their compassion? I submit that it was a short-lived concern because, after all, the job had to be done, the move had to be made and workers declared surplus had to be terminated. What choice did managers have but to get on with the job? For them, painful truths were quickly shunted aside and memories conveniently adjusted. After all, wasn't there surplus on the payroll? And weren't the employees who were sent on their way really not contributing that much anyway?

For individuals with a conscience, however, the emotional and spiritual crisis was overwhelming and debilitating. Many found the only way to survive was to anesthetize themselves, separate their minds and hearts from what they saw and heard at work, and begin to live their "real" lives somewhere else.

Some of them realized that *their* future employment was just as tenuous; they could be swept away in an instant, despite assurances from their superiors that they were vital to the business. So they began to think and plan for a way to protect themselves, growing businesses of their own. They felt that the only truth, trust and security on which they could rely would be one built for themselves.

As the 21st century opened, the economy boomed again and corporations faced a shortage of talent. How could workforces be rebuilt? The same human resources directors who were once charged with sweeping staff out the door were now expected to persuade the best and the brightest to put their faith in the corporation. Some of them countered cynicism, suspicion and fear with assurances of a spiritually supportive, secure workplace. But how real is that assurance? How much weight does the intention to tell the truth carry?

In fact, it appears that as we enter the 21st century, assurances carry very little weight. As Miroslav Volf says in *Exclusion & Embrace*, "What we have come to know we must remember, and what we remember we must tell."[7] The telling of the truth—that the slashing of workforces throughout North America was largely done without regard for the consequences beyond improving the bottom line—was rarely acknowledged.

Many corporations have nearly reached a breaking point. Where there is no credibility, no support, no joy and no truth, the corporation is empty at its core. Such emptiness will be impossible to conceal from all those involved. Whatever their current perceived level of success, it will not be sustainable for much longer. They must recapture truth, or they will wither and eventually disappear.

Paying the Price

There have always been those who look on the conduct of business as more important than anything else in life. What is particularly disturbing now is that for many people business has become everything, killing the spark of the human spirit.

As a workplace consultant who has spoken to countless individuals at every level of corporate life, I hear again and again that what is required is total commitment, total loyalty and total effort. Most workers are willing to give and keep giving, but when they begin to feel that their commitment, loyalty and effort are not being repaid in kind, then fatigue, apathy and despair set in.

Organizations today are so busy making money that they no longer have the time—or make the time—to reflect on questions of employee well-being. And well-being in organizations is not a concept that is held or sustained by the individual alone. It must have corporate support. It certainly needs the cooperation of executives and key frontline managers. In today's workplace, however, the implicit understanding between employers and employees is more likely to be that everyone is expected to look after his or her own interests. The unstated underlying assumption is that if the individual does not look after self, no one else will. In this sort of atmosphere, a sense of well-being cannot survive.

Employees who feel neglected and undervalued eventually take the lesson to heart. They begin to live each day as if the employer owes them something just for turning up. They will arrive for work at the last moment, leave as soon as possible, spend as much time as they can away from the workplace during the working day, do the minimum needed to justify their pay, and take as many sick days as possible. Employers complain and make new rules, but these efforts are generally useless until the company acknowledges and deals with the roots of the malaise.

A more ominous sign is the increase in incidents of workplace rage. As Gerry Smith, trauma counselor and author of *Work Rage*, observes, rage in the workplace often stems from lack of respect. He believes employees are very much devalued these days. Employers have high expectations both in terms of time and commitment. Because they are being bombarded, employees end up feeling like faceless numbers rather than people of value.

He points to the small signals that indicate a deep-rooted problem: a consistent lack of praise or recognition, no mentoring or guiding, dropping even the small courtesies, permitting abusive behavior, or not having an harassment policy.

Some people accept what is happening around them because they have little faith that things will ever change. They want things to change, they would like to change them, they even feel it is their responsibility to change them, but they also regard the risk of taking the first step as too great. Family responsibilities, pension rights, fear of not being able to find other employment—all these factors come into play. They close their eyes, put their souls in cold storage during working hours, and concentrate on personal survival.

Others find themselves unable to tolerate the lack of respect and unceasing demands on their lives.

Whether they stay or leave, employees pay a price in terms of their health, minds and spirits, and souls. High rates of absenteeism, stress leaves and staff turnover speak to the detrimental effects on them.

Corporations without conscience, without regard for the well-being of their employees, will find themselves on the losing end. And that end is, in my view, coming sooner than they think.

No sweeping generalization is entirely accurate, but this one, I believe, has a great deal of substance. As long as corporations are able to rely on established workers, those about 40 and older, they will be permitted to continue operating in the old business-first-and-only mode. But as that generation retires and the dot.com generation moves in, the corporations that ignore the signs of work-place distress will find themselves in serious difficulty.

The key difference is life view. The work ethic of the baby boomer generation is very different from that of the dot.coms. For the dot.coms, patience and trying to work things out are alien. Conforming to old concepts and other people's ideas of what is "right" is not on their agenda. They are far more likely to act in their own interests without a second's hesitation. "I don't even have to give you a letter of resignation. If I don't come back from lunch, assume I am no longer on the payroll."

Being Whole, Being True

What is the responsibility of the corporation? It is to enunciate its values, to make clear its ethical standards, to provide policies that incorporate them, to say and show "This is what the company holds to be true." Having made the statement, the corporation must then be willing to live with the consequences.

No corporation has the right to demand that its employees accept that what it says is true. No corporation has the right to demand that its employees adopt its ethics and values.

What *is* within the right of the corporation is to declare its values and ethics and state clearly the behaviors it believes are in keeping with them. It is the right of the corporation to require that employees observe the officially sanctioned standards of behavior. It is also the right of the corporation to dismiss employees who refuse to act within those constraints.

By the same token, it is essential for employees to understand corporate limits and to accept them or not accept them. If the required behaviors are not in keeping with their personal definitions of values and ethics, they have an obligation to discuss, suggest and even press for adjustments. But if those adjustments are not appropriate—if, for example, the majority of employees are supportive of the prevailing standards—then the dissenting employees owe it to themselves and to the corporation to go elsewhere to find an environment in which they *can* feel whole.

In the end, it is the responsibility of individuals to decide whether the values and ethics of the corporation sufficiently express their personal values and ethics. Having made the decision, individuals must then be prepared to accept the consequences.

The Moral Corporation

Respect, loyalty, commitment, trust and truth—these fine words are not just ideals for the naïve and idealistic. They are the guiding principles that form the foundation of the spiritually sustaining workplace. They are core requirements for any corporation that hopes to carry on into the 21st century.

Enlightened corporations will never hesitate to show in words and in actions that their guiding principles, their ethics and standards, are strongly held and secure. They will succeed because they are honest. They will thrive and survive because they are founded on a deep belief in and commitment to truth and trust. They will live their values and beliefs sincerely, openly and lovingly.

"That which comes after
ever conforms to that
which has gone before."

Marcus Aurelius,
Meditations, IV

CHAPTER 3

The Toxic Workplace

C ompanies get exactly the people and profits they deserve, says Jeffrey Pfeffer, the Thomas D. Dee Professor of Organizational Behavior at the Stanford Graduate School of Business and author of *The Human Equation: Building Profits by Putting People First.* In an interview with David Rousseau published in *Fast Company*[8] Pfeffer said he believes employers who treat people poorly experience low rates of productivity and high rates of turnover and invariably complain about the death of loyalty and the dearth of talent. But loyalty is not dead; it is being killed by toxic workplaces that drive people away.

"The greater mystery is why management finds declining loyalty to be a mystery," says futurist Joseph F. Coates.[9] "Everyone knows why loyalty is in decline. How many times do you kick the dog before the dog shrinks back into the corner and no longer licks your hand when you come into the room?"

What is a toxic workplace? How does it affect workers' lives, relationships and health? Can we find a solution that will alleviate the pain, confusion and anxiety that result from working in a toxic environment?

The Lifeless Workplace

Pfeffer's definition of a toxic workplace is "a place where people come to work so they can make enough money so they can leave it."

My definition of a toxic workplace is one without honest human relationships. It has nothing to do with the physical environment or sick-building syndrome. It has everything to do with lack of truth in committing to what is important for the wholeness and well-being of employees. It is a workplace filled with people who are not truly alive because the organization itself is not truly alive. The lack of life is often very subtle and difficult to detect because it is driven by fear, an emotion most people will go to any lengths to conceal.

Like many people today, I have experienced the toxic workplace firsthand. One of the most egregious examples was a large clothing manufacturer with operations in both Canada and the United States. It was a fear-based environment dominated by a general manager who was constantly verbally abusive, negative and disparaging. The manager's staff was totally demoralized and apprehensive because they never knew when he was going to subject them to an emotional outburst, harsh and unwarranted criticism, and other destructive behavior that was unacceptable by anybody's standards.

Why did the staff tolerate it? They were totally committed to the product, which was recognized and acclaimed internationally. They were totally committed to the owner of the company. Also, key management jobs in the fashion sector were hard to find.

Did any of the workers consider going to the owner and reporting the situation? I believe not. The consensus was that the general manager was so brilliant and so creative that his behavior simply had to be tolerated. It was the price employees felt they had to pay to work with someone who was perceived as a genius in an industry they loved.

Was the age of the workforce a factor? That is unlikely. The workers ranged in ages from 23 to 60.

As for me, I was unwilling and unable to witness the situation. After a few weeks, I resigned my consultancy. I was not surprised when the company went bankrupt a few months later. The causative factor, I believe, was the toxic environment.

The connection is this: When you are so out of touch with the human element of an organization, you are, by definition, out of touch with the human spirit. And when you are out of touch with the human spirit, you will eventually kill it—and the organization with it.

When companies go bankrupt, all the usual reasons are cited—mismanagement, problems with cash flow, sudden changes in market conditions. What I find fascinating is how rarely people recognize that *fear* is often a factor lurking at the scene. Yes, at times every business, however healthy and strong it appears to be, has to make decisions that will cause disruption, pain, dis-ease, uncertainty, and even fear in its workforce. That is simply part of life. I am not suggesting that if a business has games in the morning, compliments all day and goodbye hugs at five o'clock, everything is going to be lovely, safe and profitable. What I am suggesting is that in a toxic environment there is no support for workers from management, or between workers themselves, that prepares them to deal effectively with the inevitable revised strategies, changes in direction, downsizings and reorganizations.

When I visualize the effects of a toxic workplaces, I visualize a tree. Trees are survivors at all costs. They remain standing through storms and droughts. It takes a lot to kill them. But if you put poison on the soil surrounding the tree, that poison will seep into the roots and then be pulled into the tree itself. Eventually, the tree will be so weakened that it will stop growing. Its leaves will turn yellow and drop off. In time, the smallest puff of wind will knock it down.

In toxic workplaces, the poison is spread through word of mouth, through the way the company's products and services are perceived by its customers, suppliers, associates and allies. Eventually, some emergency—perhaps a major interruption in the cash flow or the loss of a key order—will bring the business to a crisis point.

The reality is that corporations have to deal with change. But if its employees are just barely surviving, they are not going to be very adaptable. If they are having trouble handling stable conditions, how can they possibly be expected to rise to exceptional occasions? How can they possibly be expected to be creative and entrepreneurial and committed, when they are disenchanted and dis-eased? A toxic environment breeds a kind of nonresponse because it has sapped the strength and spirit from workers.

The Human Factor

About 15 years ago, I attended a workshop called Warriors of the Heart, under the leadership of the late Daanan Parry, founder of EarthStewards, of Bainbridge Island in Washington State. The participants were businesspeople with a high level of consciousness about the damage caused by toxic workplaces. We were divided into teams and given instructions about playing a game on conflict. The team that ended the game with the greatest number of team members surviving would win.

Halfway through the game, a "bomb" dropped on my team and "killed" a number of us. The survivors, including me, just carried on. We paid no attention to the loss. We were entirely focused on the competition and the need to win. Yet all of us professed to be caring, humane people with concern for our colleagues. If we could not be caring and humane even in the context of a game, what can we expect of people caught up in real-life concerns?

I think this experience illustrates some important realities about human beings. One is the power of social conditioning. We are all very much shaped and pushed by circumstances, our expectations for ourselves and the expectations of others. I think it also illustrates something intrinsic in human nature. Whether or not we realize it, whether or not we accept it, competition, the desire to win at nearly any cost, is a powerful, primeval force. It is not that we want to harm others or see others harmed, but there is a force within us that permits us to tolerate and even accept harm to others in the pursuit of other rewards that seem more important.

This force is virtually undetectable. It is like the poison spread on soil around the tree. It seeps underground where it remains unnoticed. The tree remains standing. If we do not see evidence of the damage, we do not have to pay attention to it. Yet all that time, the tree is standing in poisoned ground and drawing in the toxin.

In a toxic workplace, the poison, the dis-ease, is rarely seen and rarely recognized. Few people will take the time to really examine the environment. All that matters are the visible, surface signs. The profit picture looks good. The CEO is articulate. Everyone says this is a wonderful company. Why would anybody question what the company is giving back to its employees? But eventually that toxic company is going to exhaust its human potential.

Toxic Characteristics

The toxic corporation is focused exclusively on short-term productivity and profits without equal concern for the hearts and souls of its workers.

As we enter the 21st century and as the knowledge economy matures, I believe we are carrying with us an attitude toward an employee as a dispensable, replaceable tool rather than a human being with a soul, spirit and heart. The toxic environment is becoming the standard rather than the exception. Truth*less*ness and dishonesty are poisoning the implied social contract between employers and employees.

If employers who really do care only for bottom-line results are truthful and honest, they will say so. The employees then have an opportunity to understand the nature of the choice. The workplaces may be unpleasant, but they are not, strictly speaking, toxic.

If employers who really do care only for bottom-line results are *not* truthful, they will present themselves as being caring and concerned and thoughtful about their employees as human beings. The employees do not have an opportunity to understand the nature of the choice. The workplaces are toxic by definition.

When I speak of toxic corporations and toxic workplaces, I refer to places that take much more than they ever give back. And one of the things they never give back are truthful choices, including a choice about how workers relate to one another.

Some years ago, I worked for Eaton's of Canada. (This company went bankrupt in 1999.) As a senior buyer, I was expected to attend staff meetings regularly. What I saw, felt and heard was immense pressure to "make your numbers" at any cost. The corporate culture promoted and encouraged intense, although healthy, competition between departments.

I was put in charge of buying stock for a newly formed department. My mandate was to draw on suppliers as I wished, including suppliers of lines currently represented in a number of existing departments. Naturally, some of the other buyers reacted negatively. They had worked hard to develop relationships with their suppliers, and now I was reaping the benefit.

Forming this new department made great sense; in fact, it was a necessary evolution. Drawing on existing lines and crossing departmental boundaries made great sense too. The problem was that there was very little communication or preparation to help the buyers understand the change. By not taking appropriate care with the human element, the company jeopardized the move. The business decision was the right one, but the execution was poor.

In this type of environment, workers are inevitably going to respond in ways that are not necessarily in keeping with their own

truth, spirit, or soul. The need to survive will override other consid-
erations. What happens when the boss comes in and announces that
the employee has just hours to pull something important together
and it had better be brilliant? That employee is going to react differently from the way he or she would in an environment where the
day-to-day atmosphere fosters respect, reason and mutual support.

If employers make constant demands without any consideration
for workers' circumstances and well-being, will they get the best? If
they encourage employees to fight each other, will they get the
results they want? For a time, perhaps, but not likely *over* time.

Toxic workplaces are managed by manipulation. The public
message may be that employees are a valued resource, that they
receive superior benefits, that they are nurtured, that no effort will
be spared to treat them with dignity and respect. But the fact is that
in toxic workplaces employees are not consulted, not listened to, not
heard and not cared about.

Is it realistic to expect any corporation to make every one of its
5,000 or 55,000 employees feel valued and nurtured? No, it is not
humanly possible. But it is possible to help employees learn to deal
with their fears and anxieties and to become supportive team players. In a toxic workplace, this never happens. Employees are told to
do their jobs and make the bottom line. They are well aware that
they may be marginalized no matter how good they are or how hard
they work.

I believe that regardless of the size of the workforce, it is the
responsibility of corporate leaders to honor and support the employees working on their teams. It is up to the corporations' managers to
ensure that employees know they are truly valued and respected.
The task is a difficult one. It takes committed, clear-sighted and
secure individuals to provide this leadership in any working environment, toxic or otherwise.

I believe one of the great challenges facing 21st-century corporations is that of changing their entire approach—to strategic planning,

to human resources development, to day-to-day operations. They must decide whether they are going to hold on to their values under fire. If they do not, they jeopardize much of what they have built and represent.

Action, Reaction
Toxic or healthy? Who creates it?
Who is responsible?

People bring their characters, emotions, experiences and attitudes with them to the workplace. Whether techno-peasants or CEOs, it is their responsibility to park their personal issues at the door. Realistically speaking, this is seldom possible to do with complete success. People are human. They will inevitably bring personal problems to the workplace. Even given the best will in the world, these personal problems will impinge on the atmosphere and circumstances in which people work. Everyone around them will be affected—they may not be affected directly; they may be affected only to a very small degree, but they will be affected.

Having said that, I believe both CEOs and frontline managers are collectively responsible for the character and well-being of the workplace. It is their responsibility to provide a healthy work environment. It is their responsibility to ensure that employees can do their work in an atmosphere of respect and confidence. It is also their responsibility to recognize toxicity and deal with it quickly and effectively to maintain a healthy workplace.

If employees bring abusive or otherwise harmful behavior into the workplace, it is the corporation's responsibility to do something about it. That may simply mean ensuring that an employee gets professional treatment or stress leave. It may mean terminating an employee. Taking action will not necessarily solve the problem immediately and for all time. There will often be lingering effects because employees' confidence and morale may be shaken.

But the price of *not* taking action—burying heads in the sand, turning backs, trivializing or dismissing—is a guarantee that the toxicity will fester and spread. If left unchecked, the result will be devastating physical, mental or emotional damage that can be costly to the corporation.

By the same token, employees must carry a share of the burden. It is their responsibility to report toxic behaviors to their managers or to someone in a position of authority in the workplace. If they think a co-worker has a problem, they should ask for help in dealing with the problem.

What if the worker is mentally unbalanced? Surely the employer cannot be held responsible for that! No, the employer cannot be held responsible for the worker's mental illness, but the employer can—and should—be held responsible for ignoring the signals or for not taking effective action to help the worker and protect other employees.

Good Intentions, Bad Results

Employers are not responsible for making employees well and healthy persons. But they are responsible for making a lively and healthy organization in which employees can work without corrosive fear or anxiety.

Most corporations have lofty ideals about how they want to be perceived, and many managers are prepared to work with respect and courtesy. However, far too many companies tolerate or even subtly encourage the use of fear and anxiety as tools useful for manipulating their workforces.

For example, what if a well-intentioned worker respects his or her colleagues and does good work and works in a happy, harmonious section that is virtually separate from the rest of the organization? Whenever that worker has to deal with outsiders, meaning employees from other parts of the company, he or she detects signs of toxicity. (See the list of signs below.) What is that worker's responsibility?

Five Signs of Toxicity in the Workplace

1. Lethargy
2. Absenteeism
3. Verbal and physical intimidation
4. Sexist or racist comments
5. Foul language

Some people would say that the worker should just concentrate on keeping his or her section happy and harmonious—never mind what is happening in other sections. I believe the worker has a responsibility to report a disruption to someone in authority. It may be a human resources professional; it may be someone else. It is important, however, that the person be someone the worker trusts.

Still, in these situations both managers and workers face a dilemma. The choices are not always as clear-cut as we would like them to be. For managers, the alternatives are to pay attention to the whistle-blower or impose silence by doing whatever is necessary, up to and including terminating the whistle-blower. After all, killing the messenger who brings bad news is a centuries-old tradition. For the workers, the alternatives are to report the signs of toxicity and risk being fired, or concentrate on keeping their heads down and carrying on as usual.

A truly concerned whistle-blower is a risk-taker. Corporations need risk-takers, who are also more likely to be innovative, creative and entrepreneurial. At the same time, employers tend to fear risk-takers because although they may be reliable, they are often unpredictable.

There is another aspect of the dilemma for employers. Employees who accept the status quo because it is easier, who avoid rocking the boat at any cost, who shun conflict or even the slightest possibility of conflict, are likely to be less innovative, creative and entrepreneurial.

But they are also likely to be predictable, and predictability is something on which every corporation relies to one extent or another.

So another dimension of the dilemma for managers is whether it is wise to keep the whistle-blower, because his or her very presence will present the possibility of conflict and turmoil, something the status quo-ers cannot tolerate. Status quo-ers keep the day-to-day operations running, day in and day out. Whistle-blowers—risk-takers—may choose to leave the corporation anyway because that is their nature—to take risks.

Another common dimension of the dilemma applies to both workers and managers. What should they do when they can identify a particular person as the toxic element? If the toxic individual is very senior or highly valued for some other reason, colleagues may decide to tolerate or work around the problems, no matter how much discomfort that individual brings to the atmosphere.

My position is that while the choices may not be as clear-cut as we would like, we do have a clear, guiding principle. That principle is our responsibility to create and maintain a healthy workplace in which everyone is treated with respect, may work in safety and without undue fear and anxiety, and is dealt with truthfully and honestly. It is never acceptable to fire someone for being the messenger who brings the bad news. It may be appropriate to fire a risk-taker or a status quo-er, but only for truthful, clearly explained reasons.

For individuals within the corporation—whether employees or managers—the stakes are always high. They must surely ask themselves how much they can reasonably be expected to do. Isn't it enough to keep their parts of the corporation happy and working well? Isn't it enough to deal honestly and honorably with their co-workers?

Just as no single individual can save the world, it is unfair to think that an individual can save a corporation. But every individual is part of the corporation's root system that keeps the corporate tree standing. That tree will stay standing only as long as the employees continue to be honest and honorable in order to maintain a healthy workplace. As Gene F. Hensley, executive vice-president of Trendwest Resorts, Inc. in Seattle, says, "Good for the sake of good will have the greatest return in the long run."

Signs and Portents

Gerry Smith, trauma counselor and author of *Work Rage: Identify the Problems, Implement the Solutions*, defines work rage this way: "Workplace rage is any physical assault, behavior considered to be threatening or abuse in a verbal manner that occurs in the work setting."[10] He cites examples ranging from physical altercation to homicide.

Recognizing a toxic workplace is usually easier in retrospect than it is during the fact. It is unlikely, for example, especially in a major corporation, that all employees will be unhappy to the extraordinary degree that makes toxicity apparent and visible. But the cumulative effect of toxic conditions is extremely damaging, and the cost— human and financial—very high.

"The cost can be measured in increased blood pressure, strokes and heart attacks and *karoshi,* the Japanese word for sudden death from overwork that joined the English lexicon in 1997," says Heather Menzies, author of *Whose Brave New World?*[11]. She goes on to say, "Bill Wilderson, cofounder of the Canadian Business and Economic Roundtable on Mental Health, says work-stress related depression is the disability issue of the 21st century, costing North American business in the order of $60 billion a year."

How does the downslide to systemic toxicity start? One of the smallest signs is the rise in complaints. Grumbling in the workplace is very common; there will always be people who are not happy, who feel their colleagues and employers owe them perfect comfort and contentment, and who are quick to find fault with and ascribe every personal failure or disappointment to others. It is easy—and tempting—to dismiss them as malcontents. Sometimes it is justified.

When the grumbling becomes endemic, however, it is likely that serious anxieties are bubbling beneath the surface. When the number of sick days starts to balloon beyond expected norms, when the number of employees experiencing symptoms of prolonged stress starts to mushroom, when personality conflicts start to increase in frequency or seriousness, it is imperative that the causes be identified and the effects addressed quickly and effectively.

What seem to be minor changes in behavior are often the earliest warning of dysfunctionality taking hold. For example, formerly pleasant, cheerful and cooperative employees start to look unhappy or withdrawn. Employees who used to operate with confidence and initiative seem to lose their edge. Colleagues who used to get along start snapping at or ridiculing each other. Workers who could be counted on to do that overtime or change personal plans to meet urgent deadlines start displaying a marked reluctance. Turf wars become common. Company social functions become something to be avoided rather than welcomed. Are these symptoms due to individuals' personal problems, or are they a sign of deeper distress?

Loss of self-confidence and initiative in an individual is a symptom that should never be ignored. Some may undoubtedly be the result of personal problems peculiar to the individual. Even so, problems like these should be addressed because the result can be damaging to the company as well as to the individual. Managers must be trained to step in with care, and their training must be kept up to date. The company should also set up or arrange for a trauma team to be ready at a moment's notice if a crisis, such as a serious incident of work rage, occurs.

They will find identifying and dealing with toxicity challenging because of the power of the negative. Negative environments feed on negativity. When negativity becomes the norm, it infects and destroys the good and the healthy. People with life, spirit and energy will find themselves stymied and drained by those who have accommodated themselves to the negative atmosphere and resent anyone trying to change it.

The Skill of Discernment

A few years ago I was dealing with an internationally known brokerage house. One morning, a long-standing employee dropped dead at work. Naturally, everyone was shaken by the experience. What struck me was that everyone went back to work that same day. After all, the Dow Jones was in the midst of breaking another record. No one had time to waste grieving.

A week later, I learned that few had gone to the funeral, few had enquired about the man's family, and no one had talked about the experience, at least to colleagues. It was as if the man had never existed and the traumatic event had never occurred. I was reminded strongly about my Warriors of the Heart workshop experience.

I do not believe that these people were unfeeling or unmarked by the death of their colleague. I do believe that they existed in an environment that did not permit them to consider anything beyond very narrow confines. I also believe that they were so bound up in the straitjacket of business-first-and-last, they had lost sight of their own humanity.

Recognizing and dealing with the concept of humanity is going to be one of the most demanding and urgent needs in the 21st-century workplace. The key skill is the skill of discernment—the quality of good judgment. By this I mean the ability to clearly distinguish between reality and our perception of reality.

Excercising discernment in the living workplace certainly enables a positive atmosphere that supports intuition and feelings. But human feelings are not always welcomed or accepted in the workplace as valid or important. Women are sometimes encouraged to be intuitive, sensitive and feeling beings. But they are also often dismissed as illogical and too soft for the rough-and-tumble business world. Hard logic is held as the superior benchmark. Both men and women are expected to be logical, hardheaded and factual.

Judgment based on gut feel is deemed unreliable, despite evidence to the contrary.

Discernment and intuition are the basis for self-understanding and self-actualization. Any successful entrepreneur will testify to that. If your stomach is twisted into knots and you dread going to work every day, no matter what reason indicates, something is wrong. Listing the pros and cons is not necessarily going to relieve the anguish.

For individuals who have been trained to resist inner impulses or who have been told they have to toughen up, it is difficult to avoid experiencing doubt and an erosion of self-confidence. Those who are sustained on a spiritual level may well be in a better position. Those who have a religious faith that provides the comfort of a belief in something greater than themselves or their immediate circumstances may find it easier to deal with the apprehension, fear and anxiety that permeate a toxic workplace.

What 21st-century workers need to do is learn to look at life from a broader perspective. If they are going to survive as whole human beings, if they are going to protect or salvage their souls and spirits, they are going to have to examine their circumstances with courage and determination. All individuals will have to take responsibility for looking with clear eyes and whole hearts at where they are and where they want to be, what their lives are and what they want their lives to be, what they want to change and what they *can* change. This most certainly will give them the inner strength, awareness and understanding that will protect them from the power of negativity.

The Fear Factor

One of the greatest human fears is fear of the unknown. For many workers, the way to cope has been to find a form of equilibrium. The working environment may be unpleasant, difficult or even downright unbearable, but these employees have found a way to get through every day. It has the comfort of familiarity. Better the devil you know than the devil you don't. The balance, however, is tenuous and easily disturbed.

This is another challenge for corporations concerned about symptoms of toxicity and determined to make positive changes. They are likely to find that however good their intentions, their plans are met with resistance. Inevitably, employees are going to wonder how the changes will affect them, how they are going to be expected to change, and what the risks of change are. Having anesthetized themselves in order to cope, they are going to resist being prodded to life again for reasons not easily explained. One is that change with unknown consequences is viewed as spelling danger.

This deeply ingrained fear is a force that perpetuates toxicity in the workplace. Refusing to admit natural human feelings, and tolerating the negative on the grounds that it is the only way to survive, deadens the human spirit. The pressure, often irresistible, is to keep going at any cost because the potential consequences of questioning are too frightening to contemplate.

Conscience and Compassion

Erecting a barrier between feelings and "real life" in order to get through the day is not something peculiar to the workplace. People do it in their personal lives too.

The toxic workplace has its roots in a toxic society. How often do we sit in front of the television eating our suppers while watching reports of famine, death and destruction? *Dreadful, dreadful,* we say, as we serve dessert.

Is it realistic to hold ourselves responsible for wars and famines in far-off parts of the world? No. These things are beyond our power to change.

Is it realistic to look at our own lives and take responsibility for living them with conscience and consciousness? Yes. That *is* within our power to change. We can see what is around us. We can hold out a helping hand or give a word of comfort to a troubled colleague. We can report distress and disturbance to someone in authority. We can recognize that as important as the bottom line is, the human spirit is more important still. We can be respectful and truthful. We can assist without being intrusive or controlling. We can be. We must be. We owe it to ourselves to be compassionate human beings.

The change I see coming is a change of attitude corporations will be required to accommodate. "What is in it for me" is changing to "what is right for my soul." Whether or not individuals become consciously aware of the manipulative forces in the corporate world, they will become increasingly less responsive to those manipulations and increasingly resistant to them. And what individuals are going to demand as "what is right my for soul" will be corporations of well-being that reject toxic forces in the working environment. Individuals will question, consciously or unconsciously, whether corporations are genuine about creating and maintaining healthy, respectful environments. Individuals will look for businesses that respect human values and human feelings and that consider these as important to their operations for financial profits. Prospective employees will question motives and intentions, make judgments, and voice their displeasure with their feet. The line of acceptance and tolerance will move. It is inevitable that the pallisades of denial will be breached.

Heart and Soul

In the 21st century, the culture of the workplace will demand an awakening of a new language, and truthfulness. The question workers will ask is not what is wrong or who is to blame, but what is being done to fix the problems, break the habit of manipulation and ease the weight of control. Workers will seek a spirit-driven workplace.

Visionary CEOs already fully understand the advantages of a solid, engaged workforce, recognize the beneficial effects on the bottom line, and are changing their approach to one more in tune with the culture of what I call the Age of Possibilities.

In "Leveraging Corporate Performance through Human Capital Profiling," Dr. Rich Handley compares the old business model of the Industrial Revolution with the new business model of the Information Age: "The basic shift is from treating business as a battlefield to treating it as an ecosystem, from treating corporations as well-oiled machines that are run, to lead, using command-and-control tactics, and from treating employees as cogs that can be replaced when necessary to improve the machine's performance. The old strategy tended to dehumanize people, treating the system itself as more important than the people who make up the system. The shift is towards viewing the company as a community, the role of management being to serve rather than control, treating employees as peers or co-owners rather than children."

But some senior business leaders are still operating within the traditional, hierarchical framework. They have yet to understand the advantages that come with being a spiritually driven organization. They know about heart, but they have not yet talked openly and frankly about the human spirit and the spiritually driven workforce. They will discover that manipulation and control ultimately destroy loyalty and commitment. They will accept the need to build a new language and a new understanding that goes beyond providing an employee assistance program for workers in distress. They will find themselves nurturing the corporate tree and enriching the soil around it. If they fail to do so, they will find themselves watching the leaves wither, the roots decay and the fruits rot and fall to the ground.

The Way Ahead

Work rage existed for a long time. It is not a new phenomenon. What seems to be changing, however, is the number and severity of incidents.

Trauma counselor Gerry Smith says, "When I first started responding to trauma (about six years earlier), there were only a few incidents every month relating to workplace violence. Today such incidents amount to more than 30 percent of our total workload. The service responds to more than 1,000 events every year—more than 300 of them related in one way or another to violence or rage in the workplace."[12]

Naturally, all of us are becoming more aware of work rage. We are hearing and reading media accounts of current work rage tragedies. As well, our intuition is telling us that everyone is at a breaking point and few are able to express their frustrations effectively and safely. It is hardly surprising that what is happening in society at large is reflected in the workplace.

Everyone, irrespective of status within the workplace, is responsible for the environment within. Everyone is accountable to a greater or lesser degree. Because we are all human beings, we have a sacred duty to treat each other as equals and with kindness. It is unacceptable to classify and distinguish human beings by the amount of money they earn, by their status in society, or by their perceived degree of success, even though these types of disparities are alive and growing.

Some argue that this view is all very well as far as it goes, but is naïve and cannot be expected to apply in the real world. They say that the *raison d'être* of the corporation is to be efficient, productive and careful with money and other resources, and to pursue growth and profit. In this scenario, the rightful position of employees is to do their jobs and keep quiet.

My view is that all the evidence—seen and unseen—shows a seismic shift in social attitude that will shake the corporation and the traditional model to its foundation.

Can we find a solution that will alleviate the confusion and distrust that arise when toxic environments take hold? Yes, but only with great difficulty. It will take enormous effort and determination on the part of everyone, from the warehouse worker to the CEO. No one is exempt. No one is powerless. No one has the right to step aside or refuse to shoulder a share of the responsibility.

In healthy environments, everyone is encouraged to be who he or she truly is. The reward for individuals will be personal growth, spiritual calm, and truthful living . The reward for corporations will be credibility, financial success, growth and a future far beyond the next quarterly results.

The path from toxic environment to a spiritually driven environment is a demanding one. The risks are huge because the effort depends on so many people, each with different perspectives. Some of them are so damaged that they have been reduced to numbness or destructive behavior.

I agree with Jeffrey Pfeffer when he says that toxic workplaces inspire employees only to make enough money to leave. I agree. If it means hanging on until they secure their pensions, that is what they will do. If it means taking antidepressants to manage the anxiety that grips them every day, resorting to alcohol and other drugs to mask their misery or venting their rage on their families, they will pay the price. If their only hope of sleeping at night is to go to bed physically exhausted, they will get on the treadmill and run until they can hardly stand. Persuading people so demoralized and beaten in spirit to scrape up enough trust to give loyalty and commitment another chance is a difficult summit to reach.

The detoxification process will be long and difficult, but it can be started with small actions, so small that they could be dismissed as inconsequential in themselves (see the list on the following page). The leadership must come from visionary and intuitive managers who are prepared to put themselves on the line. Dr. Ronald Heifetz, director of the Leadership Education Project at Harvard University's Kennedy School of Government and author of *Leadership Without Easy Answers*, is of the view that a leader must engage people in facing the challenge, adjusting their values, changing perspectives and developing new habits of behavior.

Ways to Detoxify the Workplace

1. Reconfigure workstations to be more people-friendly.
2. Ensure everyone has ergonomically designed furniture and equipment.
3. Allow individuals to bring plants and personal decorations to their workstations.
4. Where possible, redesign the physical environment to bring in natural light and fresh air.
5. Provide a quiet room for meditation and privacy.
6. Encourage mental and physical breaks.
7. Arrange lunch breaks with healthy food and interesting speakers addressing issues of current interest and value.
8. Greet colleagues with enthusiasm.
9. Share healthy humor.
10. Remember birthdays and other special occasions.
11. Say thank you often and sincerely.
12. Support charitable causes of which employees approve.
13. Encourage employees to volunteer time in the community.
14. Give awards for exceptional efforts as well as achievements both inside and outside the workplace.
15. Ask employees what they want, and address these requests as much as possible, as proof of good faith.

In my view, the effective solution will be created by people within the corporation working with the help of experienced and strategic coaches. The pace will be slow and incremental. But it will come if it is rooted in truth, in trust, in a change of behaviors, language and attitude, and with regard for the human spirit.

Will changes be made? Absolutely. Are people going to be prepared to make those changes? For some, it will be with the greatest reluctance. But the emerging spiritual worker is going to make the decision for change pretty easily. Already there are workers who are determined to emerge with their souls and spirits intact. They are no longer prepared to live in isolation and fear. They are determined to be free, and they will *make* their freedom. They will be the creators and the change-drivers. They will begin the movement by insisting on change or choosing to leave for places where they can recreate their lives according to their individual dreams and desires.

The situation can be seen as desperate, but it is not hopeless. It will never be hopeless as long as the human spirit refuses to be diminished.

"The secret of success is constancy to purpose."

Benjamin Disraeli
(1804–1881),
Speech, June 24, 1870

CHAPTER 4

Winds of Change

C hange is a word we use all the time and with about as much thought as we give to the word *love*. We love our homes, we love our cars, we change our plans, we change our minds, and so on. *Change* has become a word that is virtually meaningless. And yet it often signals profound and life-altering experiences. Sometimes it is so easily achieved, so unremarkable, that it may slip by unobserved. At other times change makes the ground beneath our feet tremble even at its most distant approach.

By definition, change is continuous and not permanent. It brings or creates uncertainty. It is surprising to me, therefore, that so many people regard change as a *fait accompli*. "I have made the change and so now it is finished." They expect a period of calm and constancy, as if between storms.

The perception is that change can be made fixed and steady. The fact is that while the results of change may be all of these things for a short time, change is constant. As Heraclitus said, "Everything flows and nothing stays."

St. James said it this way: "Why, you do not even know what will happen tomorrow. What is your life? You are a mist that appears for a little while and then vanishes."[13]

We may choose not to see the change. We may choose to focus on the little bits of our lives we can control—or feel we can control. It does about as much good as trying to ignore an elephant in the living room. Like it or not, the beast commands attention.

Making Change

About 70 percent of all business change initiatives fail, say Michael Beer and Nitin Nohria. "Few companies manage the process as well as they would like. Most of their initiatives—installing new technology, downsizing, restructuring or trying to change the corporate culture—have low success rates."[14]

Beer and Nohria, who are professors of Business at the Harvard Business School, lay this shockingly high rate of failure at the feet of managers who become enamored with the process, lose focus, are mesmerized by "an alphabet soup of initiatives," and lack understanding of the nature and process of corporate change. They believe a fundamental problem is that senior executives unconsciously limit themselves to choosing *either* Theory E (change is based on economic value) *or* Theory O (change is based on organizational capability). Beer and Nohria advise an integrated approach using both theories to simultaneously build up corporate cultures *and* enhance shareholder value, as illustrated in the table below.

Using Theory E, Theory O, and Theories E and O Combined

Dimensions of Change	Theory E	Theory O	Theories E and O Combined
Goals	Maximize shareholder value	Develop organizational capabilities	Explicitly embrace the paradox between economic value and organizational capability
Leadership	Manage change from the top down	Encourage participation from the bottom up	Set direction from the top and engage the people below
Focus	Emphasize structure and systems	Build up corporate culture, employees' behaviors and attitudes	Focus simultaneously on the hard (structures and systems) and the soft (corporate culture)
Process	Plan and establish programs	Experiment and evolve	Plan for spontaneity
Reward System	Motivate through financial incentives	Motivate through commitment—use pay as fair exchange	Use incentives to reinforce change but not to drive it
Use of Consultants	Consultants analyze problems and shape solutions	Consultants support management in shaping their own solutions	Consultants are expert resources who empower employees

Source: Beer, Michael, and Nitin Nohria. "Cracking the Code of Change," Harvard Business Review, May–June 2000, page 137.

Despite much evidence that poorly considered and executed change is self-defeating, corporate managers continue to chant the change mantra without much serious thought: Change is the norm. Change is continuous. Change is essential. Change or get left behind.

Another common attitude is that people instinctively fear and resist change. Christopher B. Galvin, chairman and chief executive officer of Motorola Inc., "wholeheartedly disagrees" with this view. "People fear the unknown and have anxiety over uncertainty. Change is certain, so the anxiety is over the personal and group ability to make the transition into a better place," he says, adding, "We can and will develop a changeable workforce at Motorola."

What is change? Who creates it? Are we really conscious of and definite about how we deal with change?

Most people do not seek change willingly. Generally, it is thrust upon them through circumstances and conditions beyond their control. As a rule, it is set squarely within the parameters of fear and a desperate desire for certainty and predictability. When people undergo change, their instinct is to reestablish the stability they once thought they had by reversing the change or lessening its impact. They hope to find peace, calm and emotional security.

Many people in the corporate world approach change in a superficial way. They talk about fundamental change, but what they mean and what they value is the *appearance* of change. No wonder workers become exhausted. It is like running in place. The pace is swift, the footing is always a bit uncertain, they are constantly adjusting their speed—and yet beneath the surface there is no fundamental change and they never move forward. They see that for all their efforts nothing has really changed, and they suspect that perhaps true change was never intended.

How one perceives change in both personal and corporate life depends on how well one understands one's own motives. To create and experience fundamental change, one must be totally aware and open to the idea of change. When change is brought about at the deepest, most heartfelt level of the human heart and soul, the result will always be life-altering in some significant, if not immediately apparent, way.

This applies to collective entities, such as corporations, just as it does to individuals. Author Margaret Wheatley addresses this concept in *A Simpler Way.* "A self changes when it changes its consciousness about itself. This is true for any system—individuals, organizations, societies. As the system develops a different awareness, this changed awareness will materialize as new responses. If it fails to assign different meaning, it will maintain itself unchanged. Thus, the source of change and growth for an organization or an individual is to develop increased awareness of who it is, now. If we take time to reflect together on who we are and who we could choose to become, we will be led into the territory where change originates. We will be led to explore our agreements of belonging, the principles and values we display in our behaviors, the purposes that have called us together, the worlds we've created."[15]

Corporations must look at change in the context of, as Wheatley puts it, "our agreements of belonging." Will the changes being contemplated result in fundamental changes to our collective understanding and implicit agreements? Or will the results be simply superficial, of no lasting consequence, and make as much of an impression as a whisper in a noisy room? Are corporations responding to employees' needs and views with *pro forma* responses, or are they being thoughtful and truthful? Twenty-first-century corporations must come to grips with the 20th-century heritage of superficiality. If they do not give proper consideration to "our agreements of belonging," they will alienate the employees on whom they depend.

Questioning Change

When I interviewed Margaret Wheatley in April 2000, she told me she believes that today we are exercising more personal freedom than ever before. She also believes that the call of the soul in today's world of work cannot be reconciled with current workplace philosophies because soul and work are pulling us in opposite directions.

Inviting change or creating change is indeed about exercising free will and making choices. If individuals are not prepared to open themselves, and be totally present and vulnerable, change can occur only on a superficial level.

Like Motorola Inc.'s Christopher Galvin, I do not believe that people in today's workplace are particularly resistant to change or intrinsically suspicious of change, when it is properly communicated. Most people in the corporate world are very accommodating to change around them. They know how to play the game, and they do so with varying degrees of enthusiasm.

However, when people in today's workplace say they accept change, often they are overlooking the deeper aspects of what *creates* change. The problem is that everybody is traveling so fast, and change is happening so rapidly, very few have time to stop long enough to figure out where they are going or what they will do when they get there.

The vast majority are far too rushed to give any thought to the nature of change and their role within it. They are never encouraged to look at change and how it will affect them and their role within the company in a deeper, more contemplative fashion. They are not allowed time to ask what the company is really doing, why it is doing it, what part individuals will play in this new living workplace, what the effects will be, whether they want to be part of it, or, most important of all, how they can contribute while maintaining their soul.

Asking these questions can be dangerous for the individual and for the corporation. If individuals ask themselves how they really feel about change, they must then go on to the next question: Do I choose to change, or do I choose to challenge the proposed change? If the answer does not conform to the collective voice, choices must be made. Every choice, including the choice of not dealing with the question, carries a price.

Says management consultant Chris Christensen, president of California-based Christensen Associates, Inc.: "Employees are not expressing their concerns regarding the changes that are occurring. Some are in denial—pretending that the future will not really demand that they make changes today. Others are so frightened by the future that they are immobilized and cannot take any intelligent action to prepare for their future in a globalized, technological age. My prediction is that many workers will wait too long to start to accept personal responsibility for their own development and they will never catch up. They will be the homeless and destitute ones in the future."

Individuals must be accountable to themselves. They must be prepared to recognize and accept change, enter consciously into the state of flux that is change, and deal with the unknown. If they refuse to think for themselves about the implications of change, they are not only abrogating a critical, personal responsibility; but also are risking their futures.

Speaking Change

Like writer and broadcaster Charles Handy, I believe language is often the herald of change.[16] How we think and speak of change directly affects our ability to create, accept and deal with it.

When I think about change, I think about creation, about caring, about commitment. I think about being conscious, compassionate and concerned. I use words like *creativity, communication, spirit, values, opportunity, courage* and *excitement.*

I believe that ideas and words like these are the very bedrock that gives individuals the ability to create and accept change. If we use positive ideas and words, we put ourselves in a frame of mind that gives us permission to act. If we use the negative, expressed by words such as *decayed, demoralized, damaged, destroyed* and *dangerous,* we put ourselves in a frame of mind that freezes us in despair. Even the tiniest shift in attitude may be the first step toward creating and dealing proactively with changes that affect our lives.

Few of us ever have to face circumstances as dreadful as those faced by Robert Ross, one of nine individuals saluted in May 2000 by Ontario's Centre for Addiction and Mental Health Foundation at the "Courage to Come Back" awards. Ross was physically, emotionally and sexually abused as a child, became addicted to heroin and alcohol at the age of 10, and spent most of his teen years living on the street. At the age of 36, he hit rock bottom. After a failed suicide attempt, he found the courage to seek treatment. He returned to school, reunited with his wife and children, and dedicated his life to helping youth, particularly young addicts and abused children. Today, when speaking to parents and students, he stresses the importance of the choices we make. His message is simple—you design your own destiny.

Ross accepted absolute change. He found within himself, and through his faith in God, the courage to deal with devastatingly powerful forces that had controlled his life for 26 years. He accepts as well that when he made the choice to undergo change, he also made the choice to face the same hurdles every day of his life. He understands that as an addict in recovery, he must make a conscious decision to stay clean every day. The memory of his acceptance speech will remain with me forever. I truly felt God's presence in him as he attested to his faith. Robert Ross personifies caring and courage. He is the living embodiment of commitment to change.

Courageous Change

In the corporate world, a common view is that people belong in one of two camps: those who change and those who *are* changed. The courageous change-driver spearheads adjustments in attitudes, mission statements and best practices. Everyone else is pulled toward change or meekly follows the leader. Whether the context for change is the individual, the family, the community, or the corporation, no matter how self-directed or independent one may appear to be, no one ever creates change without help or without being influenced by others. Ross's testimony speaks directly to another dimension of this reality: While change is a personal choice, it is never accomplished alone.

We may perceive ourselves as philosophically independent or well-armored, but the fact is that all of us are intricately connected to and strongly affected by the people around us, the words we hear, and by visual images, experiences and memories. We take our direction, our courage and our faith from this environment. If we are truthful with ourselves, we recognize that we are not the sole innovators, creators or leaders of change, just as we recognize that when we bring about change we cannot do it for ourselves alone.

Albert Einstein once said, "Only those who attempt the absurd will achieve the impossible." There are some people who attempt to create the absurd in order to achieve or create change.

There is an age-old saying to the effect that a good way to make God laugh is to make plans. In *Aurora Leigh, Book I*, Elizabeth Barrett Browning expressed it much more eloquently:

> God laughs in heaven when any man
> Says, 'Here I'm learned; this I understand;
> In that, I am never caught at fault or doubt.'

When we move to create change we may well make God laugh, because when all is said and done we have no control over a great deal in our lives. We make choices for ourselves, but it's always within a context. To understand the nature of the change we face and choices we make, we have to be aware of that context and how it is influencing us—directly, indirectly, consciously and unconsciously.

Awareness of purpose counts because only *we* can know what matters to us as individuals. Only *we* can know what is going on in our lives. Only *we* can know if we are poised on the brink of a stage of life or a momentous event that demands our energy and colors our judgment. The change itself may be set in motion by circumstances beyond our control, but how we react as individuals, the words we use and the way we think about it are *within* our control. This is what requires a presentness, a vulnerability, a strength.

Whether we are dealing with compelling personal issues or pressing workplace issues, awareness of purpose is the key to finding the courage and strength we need to meet the demands of the situation.

It is what we do with change that makes it good, bad or neutral. If we think about creating, accepting and shaping change as a way to create goodness, we find ourselves in a state devoid of negativity, recriminations, defensiveness and fear. We also find ourselves in a state of inclusiveness rather than separateness, generosity rather than selfishness, and hope rather than dread.

Leading Change

Leadership is another dimension of the demanding nature of change. How we define leadership, or whether we even consider it, speaks to our commitment to approach change from the perspective of creating goodness.

The true meaning of the word *leadership*, according to Donald T. Phillips, is itself elusive, vague and ambiguous. To understand it, he recommends studying the leadership styles of successful leaders who have demonstrated their abilities. He recommends emulating Abraham Lincoln, whose leadership style was founded on "an unshakable commitment to the rights of the individual."[17] How many of us could say the same of ourselves?

Recently, I consulted as a shadow coach with the president of a Canadian subsidiary of an American-owned company. The president, who had been in the position for about 18 months, had reorganized the company and introduced a new approach. She had hired new people. They were excited, eager, and still a little nervous because they were just getting used to each other and to her. But they were willing to step into the unknown future because they had confidence in her. She was a striking example of energetic, truthful, committed leadership.

At the 18-month mark, the president received an offer of promotion that would take her to the American head office, and bring with it significant personal advantages. The conflict she faced was how to do the best for herself, while also dealing with the changes needed by the company and supporting the team she had recruited. She was torn by the decision. She chose to accept the position but did not, for some time, openly communicate this to her staff. On the contrary, she falsely assured them that no further changes would occur to disrupt their already unsettled work environment.

This woman is a genuine leader because she created the climate, culture and inspiration for change. Without her, this necessary process may not have been started. In the end, however, the process was flawed due to the way she chose to communicate her decision to accept the position. It was disappointing to witness.

Embodying Change

In *Lincoln on Leadership,* Phillips defines genuine leaders as "…not only instruments *of* change, they are catalysts *for* change."[18]

I would rephrase it this way: A genuine leader is an instrument of change, a catalyst for change *and* the embodiment of change.

Being the embodiment of change means having a clear view of self, which I define as *presentness*. It means opening our minds and hearts. It means absorbing inspiration and wisdom from others of like values. It means finding courage and strength, and sharing this courage and strength willingly with others. It means constantly asking ourselves whether we can do better, or as Abraham Lincoln put it, "The dogmas of the quiet past are inadequate to the stormy present. The occasion is piled high with difficulty, and we must rise with the occasion. As our case is new, so we must think anew, and act anew."[19]

Embodying change means having a vision of hope. No matter how expectations change, circumstances challenge or people disappoint, genuine leaders keep the faith in their vision.

Embodying change means understanding and communicating its incremental nature. As Michelangelo chipped away at huge blocks of marble, guided by a design only he could see, so genuine leaders take small steps, one by one, along the path to the goal. The goal is itself a part of a greater vision of which the leader may see and understand only a small portion.

Embodying change means having the courage to formulate a vision and to embark on the journey without knowing where the path will lead.

Speeding Change

Some business leaders are coming to terms publicly with change. Most, however, are not discussing or considering it in any thoughtful way. It is not because they do not want to, not because they do not understand there are serious implications, and not because it is too difficult. I think it is simply because they have literally no time to deal with the enormity of change.

In *Blur: The Speed of Change in the Connected Economy*, Stan Davis and Christopher Meyer talk about "the meltdown of all traditional boundaries."[20] There are no longer clear lines "between structure and process, owning and using, knowing and learning, real and virtual." Their advice? "Stop trying to clarify it, codify it, explain it. Recognize it. Learn its new rules." In essence, their message is to learn to move at what they call the speed of blur.

This is characteristic of the new century's corporate world. We talk about the speed of change, coping with change, making better use of our time, telescoping processes to save time . . . but we do not actually talk about change as a component of life.

When reading books like *Blur*, I get a sense of *déjà vu*. It is almost like reverting to the great pre-Second World War discovery of time management. Clocking and timing were the keys to becoming more efficient. Ask only how to change, not why or where it might lead.

Chancing Change

Change is not something we discover. It is not something that exists in tangible form. We can examine it and discuss it only in terms of how we anticipate and experiment, how we move through it and come out of it, and how we ourselves are altered by it.

Change, like leadership, is an elusive concept. Although some people in a group will feel and experience it, others will remain unmoved and apparently untouched. It can even be precipitated by thoughts, ideas and words that were intended for another purpose entirely. (I have seen this happen often in my speaking career. Something I say sparks ideas and inspires people to create things entirely unrelated to my topic, possibly things totally unrelated to anything they have been doing to that point.)

To some people, this kind of spontaneous combustion means that change must happen by chance. Although many people believe in change by chance, however, I am reluctant to accept this view. As a person with a religious faith, I believe there is a greater design that exists beyond human understanding.

Precipitating Change

There is no way to actually avoid or sidestep change, but some things can distract one from seeing it or coming to grips with it. Prescription drugs, alcohol and illegal drugs can dull the impact. Change coaches, how-to programs, psychiatrists, psychologists and retreats can be used to help deal with the realities of change, but they are sometimes used as an excuse to procrastinate.

It is interesting to see, however, how perceptions of change differ with generations. Baby boomers, as a rule, still believe that they can predict and control change, at least in their personal lives. They have a huge influence by virtue of numbers and collective attitude, and they created monumental social and political changes that left lasting marks on public and private institutions, policies and programs.

In contrast, the dot.com generation seems fatalistic and more inclined to accept that change is what happens, that everything is ephemeral and that nothing matters more than personal comforts and desires. They are not yet pushing for change in the same way that the baby boomers did, but it's only a matter of time before the dot.com generation does too. As a group, they will effect marked change simply because they exist as the largest generation since the boomers. If the dot.comers are passionate about anything in a social or political sense, it is environmental issues, such as genetically modified foods, toxicity in the air we breathe and water we drink, and global concentration of corporate power. These are the issues on which we are most likely to see their initial impact.

For 21st-century corporations, the greater challenge will not be merely competing in a global marketplace. It will be adjusting to, accepting and accommodating a self-focused workforce—one that asks questions about change and assumes a right to have a say in why change should be undertaken, how much there should be and when it should occur. Incoming workers are going to want to create change in keeping with their values and their need for spiritual sustenance. As the unemployment rate drops and employees have more choices, corporations are going to find themselves pressed more and more to involve their employees and create loyalty. A decade or so from now, the 21st-century workplace is going to look and feel radically different from the workplace of today.

Bridging Change

Everybody living or working in the corporate environment must believe in, or at least accept, the values of the organization. If they do not, they will experience a sense of helplessness or surrender under the demands change makes of them. Participating willingly in change and supporting change requires everyone to be hopeful, regardless of their status in the corporate structure. People who do not accept or believe in the corporation's values will not accept the need for change, the change itself, or their ability to make any kind of meaningful choice with respect to the change.

How many managers in the 20th-century workplace bothered to

ask their employees about their personal values or whether they thought their personal values were congruent with the corporation's values? Not many.

How many corporate managers in the 21st century workplace have any understanding of the values of the dot.com generation and the generation following? Not many.

Recently, I spoke with the human resources director of a major Canadian financial institution. She said one of her biggest fears for the future was that key, senior managers had no idea what young employees and employees-to-be were thinking. How, she asked, will these managers be able to create the changes and understanding they will need to lead these new recruits effectively? What should they be doing?

My advice was to start talking directly and sincerely to the younger generation in a relaxed setting. (Using focus groups can skew results. There is a need to really connect, something that will not happen in a focus group setting.) There is no point in devising a plan for change somewhere else and then going out to sell it to the very people who will be expected to implement it. As well, any plan for change that is created without involvement, caring and creativity, and that is not phrased in the new language of change, will not work.

What they must also do is be clear about the values of the corporation and express those values explicitly as well as implicitly. Changing the values is not the question. Nor should it be the expectation. Building a bridge to those values is.

In my view, leading change successfully in the 21st-century workplace requires speaking in a new language, embodying truth, helping people understand that change is a complex thing, and being clear about corporate values and goals. What is the corporation's true mission? How much do people, integrity and authenticity really count when balanced against the need for profit?

Pacing Change

Although I believe that, by and large, most people in today's workplace are realistic enough to accept change, or at least accept the inevitability of change, there are some who resist. The reasons? They are not ready for it, not convinced of the need, do not see that it will benefit them personally, have not considered it, do not understand it or just do not want it. Sometimes, the reason is simply that they are too preoccupied with other matters. If an individual is in the midst of a personal, human drama—say, a marriage breakdown or another family crisis, such as a serious illness—being required to make even the smallest adjustment at work may be the straw that breaks the camel's back.

For corporate leaders, this task can be overwhelming. Change happens so quickly, they barely have time to think about what to do, much less consider the consequences and implications. At the same time, they must prepare the workforce to understand the need for change, the quality of the change and the reasons for the change, so as to enlist employees' co-operation and support. What leaders must do is join several different streams of change, all of which are flowing at different rates, into one. Is it reasonable to expect this?

In my view, it is reasonable to expect corporate leaders to embody change, to build a bridge to change by clearly expressing the direction of the change, and to give employees the tools they need to handle the change. In turn, it is equally the responsibility of the workforce to embody change, think through the change in personal terms and make choices that do not imperil the change for either themselves or the corporation. By this I mean that workers must, as individuals, decide whether their values can accommodate the change and whether they can support the direction of the change. If they can support the direction of the change, they have a responsibility to embody it—to support it wholeheartedly. If they cannot support the direction of the change, they have a responsibility not to impede it. They must either choose to stay and support the change, or declare themselves unable to accept the company's direction, and leave.

Either way, both parties have a responsibility when it comes to change. Both must have a real understanding as to why the change must be made and understand that the purpose of the change will, by definition, reach far beyond their individual concerns and priorities.

Loving Change

Those who have developed a capacity for love for themselves and for others have an advantage in times of turmoil and change. Having a sense of purpose, of caring for others and of faith is like wearing a life jacket in a fast-flowing river: it keeps one's head above the waterline. It gives one a sense of optimism, empowerment, order and comfort. Although it may seem to be an illusion, it is what prevents one from falling into the abyss of victimhood. It allows one to ride out change without being entirely or permanently devastated, and to come out the other side, relieved, perhaps, that the turmoil is over, but ready to pick up the pieces, to keep going forward and to continue being a willing participant and contributor in life.

The magic is in managing one's attitude toward the force of change. There is a big difference between experiencing change with love in your heart and experiencing change with fear and terror in your soul.

Those who are living without the gifts of nurturing and loving will find it harder to make the journey through troubled waters. But except in cases of serious mental illness that skews intellect and emotions, all of us still have the infinite resilience of the human spirit on which to draw for support and strength.

One might conclude that the most successful leaders of change would, therefore, be those who are nurturing, compassionate and caring. However, even those who have emerged from the ashes, who have not had these gifts, are still capable of leading change success-fully, as long as they are capable of opening their hearts and minds.

Nurturing Change

Successful, effective change rests on truth and hope. Truth and hope cannot flourish in an atmosphere of fear or distrust. Ultimately, both the corporation and every individual within the corporation—whether leader or follower—are responsible for change and account-able to each other for change. They share a responsibility to nurture the corporate entity and the individuals within it by sharing strength and support.

The ability for a corporation to change is directly related to the atmosphere within the organization. A loving atmosphere supports change. A fearful atmosphere works against change.

Rocky Mountain Railtours, a Vancouver-based, internationally recognized company led by Peter Armstrong, is an example of a company that truly cares about its employees. As a consultant to the company over five years, I watched Armstrong, a man of deep personal integrity, demonstrate his caring and loyalty for his employees time and again. In return, he expects, and receives, will-ingness to change, commitment and professionalism from his staff. I also watched him change the company from one with high staff turnover to one with very low turnover, as his employees responded to changes he made in his own leadership style.

I remember clearly our discussion about changing course. His view was that we choose our courses of action because we are quite certain that this is the only path to be followed. But sometimes we come to a dead end. The important thing, he says, is to ignore the dead end and to try a second and a third road if necessary. There is no point in wasting time in frustration and anger, or in agonizing over the fact that the choice did not work. A change in direction has to be communicated, but the main effort must be directed toward finding the right path.

The risk, of course, is in leaving confused people behind. Changing direction is not the problem. Not communicating it properly will be. It is important to move forward without wasting any time. But people need to know why the changes are being made in a way they can embrace. Have they been informed intelligently? Will they accept that what they have been no longer matters as they start on the new road? And do they understand that although you believe this is going to be the right road, it may not be? There is always a chance that still another change in direction will be required.

It is important to acknowledge to employees the fact that an earlier direction might not have been the right one. Not acknowledging erroneous decisions after the fact leads to confusion, frustration and cynicism among the employees on whom the CEO is counting to carry the corporation to the next stage. They are not going to be there with wholehearted commitment if the message one week is Total Quality, the next week Management by Objectives, and the week after that Cross Functional Teamwork—all without discussion, reflection or explanation.

Not telling employees what they need to hear about coming change or change already in process is counterproductive in another way. In the absence of information, people devise their own explanations. However fanciful these explanations might be, they become accepted as absolute fact. They grow in certainty like ripe grapes on the vine. A memo from management denying rumors does not solve the problem. Only if management lays cards on the table and comes clean quickly can there be any hope of quashing rumor and uncertainty.

Management can successfully execute sudden changes when it acknowledges bewilderment and creates a supportive atmosphere. Contrast Rocky Mountain Railtours with a telecommunications company, also based in western Canada, where fear is tangible. This company (Company A) merged with another company of comparable size (Company B), but Company A was clearly the dominant party. It embarked on reorganizing and rationalizing with gusto, but without bothering to tell employees what was going on or what was likely to happen to their jobs. The employees at Company B spent months waiting for the next news hurricane to hit. Very few were given the opportunity to be part of the planning for change. As a result, all of them found the situation frustrating, difficult and damaging.

Asking Change

Many corporate workers tie themselves up in the complexities of change—defining, reacting, identifying, containing, implementing. What they fail to grasp is that when one looks at change from an individual point of view, it is often essentially simple and straightforward—for example, being asked to do 15 tasks each day rather than 12 or grouping or approaching those 12 tasks in a different way.

As a result, leaders of change often have a difficult time understanding why some employees who are being asked to do very little react so negatively. One can almost see managers visibly gathering patience; what really perplexes them is why an employee seems so overwhelmed. "Come on, work with us on this. It's not a life-or-death situation."

Fear of change is often the result of hidden factors such as those listed below. Managers do not probe for the source of their employees' unrest because they do not want to hear the answer. If they hear the answer, they may be expected to do something outside of the usual corporate boundaries and expectations.

An example: A good worker who has always done a good job has a seriously sick mother at home. One day the worker's manager says, "We are giving you the opportunity to take on additional responsibilities effective immediately. We are confident that you are willing to take them on because you are so valuable to this organization and because we appreciate you."

Resistance to Change

Hidden factors may manifest themselves as fear of change. Here are some examples:

1. Resentment of colleagues (for example, a belief that others' workloads are lighter)
2. Envy of what are seen as undeserved rewards given to others
3. Concern for stability of employment or career prospects
4. Personal fatigue, or family worry, stress or illness

The problem for the worker is that he or she may be unable to absorb the additional responsibilities due to domestic pressures. The worker feels overwhelmed and responds with an emotional outburst, expressing absolute inability to accept the additional responsibilities.

What does a manager do in these circumstances? In a company of integrity, the manager will offer whatever support is available and appropriate. In a company where there is fear, the manager will simply say, "I hope you can find a way to deal with it. Let me know if I can help." The manager may also offer the bare minimum consistent with labor legislation, or whatever is needed to avoid potential, negative publicity because that is the company's policy.

Does the spirit in which support is offered make a difference to workers as long as they get the support they need when they need it? Is the best course of action simply to accept the support at face value and not question employers' motives? Genuine support offered from genuine caring is very different from *pro forma* support offered to avoid negative talk around the water cooler. Individuals have a responsibility to develop and use their intuitive skills and to guide themselves accordingly.

Advising Change

Recently, I facilitated a strategic planning session for a public utility in the United States. The utility was going through the deregulation process. The unionized workers, who formed the majority of the workforce, chose to accept management's decision to do everything without consulting the workers either directly or through the union. The union accepted its role as detached observer.

This is not unusual. There are many in the corporate world who stand aside. They see what is happening, they can explain it, they can articulate it, they can be persuasive about it—but they refuse to engage as catalysts or innovators. Instead, they stand safely on the riverbank. Some choose to stay silent. Some choose to tell those who are helpless in the roiling waters what they should do and how they should do it.

Do we need observers of change who can give advice and counsel to workers who are in the thick of it? Yes, but in my view, such observers must be people who have experienced change, who understand fear and who have intimate, personal knowledge about the barriers to change. The wisdom of the detached observer is of limited or questionable value if it has not been steeped in and shaped by life-altering change.

It is very easy to distinguish the *detached* observer from the *survivor* observer. No one who has been battered by the river, swept over the rocks, and then lived to tell the tale will ever say, "I am never going near that water again. From now on, it is do as I say, not as I do." Anyone who has survived the experience is usually much more able to contemplate the ebb and flow with equanimity, and plunge in again after a period of rest and recuperation.

Survivor observers have a responsibility to support, respect and succor those still in the river, by sharing their life experiences and giving of their wisdom and practical assistance. In my experience, survivor observers, such as battle-scarred entrepreneurs, are the first to offer a helping hand, an encouraging word and any other support possible.

Feeling Change

Given some time for personal conversation, people who have been battered by life's forces and circumstances will always find common understandings, regardless of differences in economic or social status or any other divider. Given open hearts and minds, their souls will touch as they sense a bond.

But for souls to touch, people must be very present and allow themselves to be vulnerable. If they close their minds and hearts, if they deny the life-changing experience, if they refuse to discuss it, hear it, see it or even think about it, they will block not only common understandings, but also their potential for experiencing positive future change.

Because loving involves others, however, it is difficult for people who are in a loving state to shut down their emotions and close themselves up against comfort and support. If one is in a loving state, it is impossible to close one's heart, mind and soul. It is impossible to refuse to feel suffering or painful moments in life, just as it is impossible to refuse to feel joy. A loving heart brings with it the knowledge that one is not alone.

For many people, religious faith is the ultimate source of loving comfort and strength. For others, it may be faith in the human spirit, a belief that intrinsic good is intrinsically valuable, deep roots within the community, or some other deeply held personal conviction.

Corporate Change

Change in the corporate context is nearly always justified in terms of profit, power and influence. In the second half of the 20th century, thanks to the baby boomers and their determination to exercise social conscience, corporations sometimes made a point of demonstrating community support for and participation in cause-related programs.

The evolving search for change in the corporate world is gradually coming into focus as a competition between concern for private profit and concern for social good. In the living workplace of the 21st century, success will be defined in a different way, one much more in keeping with the 19th-century view. As Edward Carpenter (1844–1929) said in *Pagan and Christian Creeds*, "The first condition of social happiness and prosperity must be the sense of the Common Life."

In the living workplace, the gap between the haves and the have-nots will not necessarily be one of differences in economic or social status. It is much more likely to be a gap between those who believe that caring for others is an essential component for a civilized society and those who find discussion over caring for others in any broad sense—a social conscience—meaningless drivel.

The new generation workers will find themselves facing a decision about whether to be fearless, courageous agents of change or to lose themselves in the existing corporate culture.

A highly respected human resources consultant thinks that profit will continue to control the corporate agenda. In a recent communication, she told me this story.

> Last fall [1999], I joined a dot.com start-up because it had a business plan that made sense and a business concept I felt would work really well on the Internet. After four months, I quit. My short answer is because values, ethics, principles and

respect for human beings matter a whole lot to me. I was working with a bunch of guys who only saw dollar signs and who would do anything that they believed was expedient to line their pockets . . . . My biggest fear is for the young kids—the hotshots fresh from university and into their first jobs at companies like this. I fear for our world because these young, somewhat impressionable "first jobbers" will believe that this is how the business world works—a world where principles, ethics, values and respect for human beings are things that are totally expendable in search of the latest dot.com million.

Although her story is disheartening, my prediction is that the majority of new workers *will* ultimately choose corporate environments where conscience coexists with profit and *will* opt to be agents for change. As a generation, they have already declared personal quality of life to be of paramount value. I believe they will take the steps to embody that value in their professional lives in ways that go beyond the purely personal.

But will they win over those who count profit and power as the ultimate arbiters? The question deserves to be considered, but I do not believe the answer is obvious. The 21st-century workplace is part of the expanding global marketplace, where individuals are making huge amounts of money and corporations are pressing for more and more control. Where do individuals with social conscience fit? How much influence do they have over ego and greed? Will they be able to exercise a collective voice?

Inspiring Change

In *Thinking in the Future Tense: Leadership Skills for a New Age*, Seattle-based cultural anthropologist Jennifer James writes, "In times of change, a moral compass is the one thing that will point you in the direction you want to go."[21]

What, then, can individuals do, not only to enable change but also to move change in a positive direction in a corporate environment where ego and greed are significant barriers?

In *The Hungry Spirit,* Charles Handy points to the social entrepreneur as the harbinger of change: "[Charles Leadbetter in *The Rise of the Social Entrepreneur*] argues that the British tradition of welfare must not be abandoned, but it must be changed. Social entrepreneurs are the harbingers of that change, devising new ways to provide support and development for those excluded from the opportunities of the new society."[22]

There have always been harbingers of change working against the odds. A contemporary example is the program in New York City that takes homeless drug addicts off the street, gives them counseling and support to battle their addictions, and trains them to do useful, publicly needed work (including sweeping streets). The results are very encouraging, and the success rate—measured in terms of whether participants stay clean and become self-supporting—is impressive.

We are all inspired by stories like these because they offer evidence that change is not just about profits. It is also about human, social and environmental issues. It is about changing our world in a way that improves the quality of life for everybody, not just for ourselves and our families.

As individuals we owe it to ourselves to reflect on change, to create change, and to recast ourselves, our institutions and our society in a way that supports the human capacity for love, trust, respect and integrity.

"Private Enemy
Number One is fear."

*John A. Redhead,
Putting Your Faith
to Work*

CHAPTER 5

Name That Fear

I came face-to-face with absolute fear in a moment of truth. I did
not seek it. It was thrust upon me when I was suddenly diagnosed
with a terminal illness. At that instant, I understood fear in a way
that, even now, years later, I can barely begin to describe. For me,
the visual image of paralyzing fear is an intensely black, airless
tunnel. No one would willingly go into such a tunnel, but some of
us are dragged into it.

In my moment of truth, I understood I had control over nothing.
But I had tenacity and a grim determination to survive. I still had
absolutely no control over the outcome. It was stunning and devastating. I lost everything but my will to live. But in the end, the experience was a gift.

Most North Americans are blessed, in the sense that by and large,
they are able to live their lives in peace and freedom. But whether
we admit it or not, whether we name it or not, fear can seep into
every part of our lives. Although we may not have a startlingly clear

and devastating epiphany, all of us experience the pain and confusion of fear. It is an inevitable part of life.

The reality and inevitability of fear forces all of us to face some questions. Do we find the courage to look into the tunnel? Do we take the initiative to walk through it of our own accord? Or do we deny its existence at all costs, even as we are being dragged inexorably toward it? How does fear change us? What price do we pay within our souls? How can we pull ourselves free from the force of fear?

The Force of Fear

Fear is a destructive force that manifests itself in many forms in today's workplace. Its presence paralyzes workers' creative and intuitive abilities and blocks their personal and professional development. Unfulfilled corporate promises and lingering, unresolved workplace issues contribute to the corrosion because they erode trust.

Like love, fear is rarely acknowledged in the workplace. As Paul Birch, director of Runston Consulting Ltd. in England, says, "Fear is rarely acknowledged because those who generate fear [those who run the company] see fear in positive terms rather than the picture seen by those who are scared. If they acknowledge it then it is usually only to pay lip service to it before dismissing it."

Everyone is expected to put on a public face that says, "Everything is fine. I am confident. I am in control. I am moving ahead." To suggest, however, that fear is not alive and thriving in today's workplace is disingenuous at best and a direct denial at worst. Fear pervades our workplaces and our daily lives. We are beset by uncertainty, the looming unknown and feelings of being vulnerable and without control.

Fear can also be used as a crutch. There are people who use fear, consciously or unconsciously, to explain—at least to themselves—why they cannot deal with their own inadequacies, failures or resistance to change.

Acknowledging Fear

During a recent session with a group of senior managers, we talked about how workplaces could be changed through good leadership. When I brought up the subject of fear, everyone froze. I had committed a serious corporate *faux pas*. There was a long moment of unbroken, uncomfortable silence. Eventually, the conversation started again. No one in that room admitted to ever feeling fearful. But each admitted to seeing fear among their associates and within their workplaces.

So, fear exists. It is an inescapable part of the human condition. But how can we find solutions if we refuse to *admit* that it exists? How can we learn to deal with fear? Where can we learn to cope with uncertainty and the unknown? Who will teach us to adapt when everything around us appears to be shifting, swirling, unpredictable change?

Most people, other than those addicted to the adrenaline generated by fear, just try to live their lives in peace. They want to live with some reasonable assurance that they will not have to deal with tragedies in the workplace or their homes. They close their eyes to fear because they know instinctively that coming to terms and dealing with it can be one of the most singularly unpleasant experiences in life.

From my perspective, having survived the journey through the tunnel of fear, the most encouraging news I have is that intense, life-changing fear will not—cannot—last forever *and* it can bring a whole new perspective. I describe it as coming to a state of knowing.

Unless we face fear head-on, we will always remain in a state of disconnectedness, and feel pain and anxiety buried deep within. We will remain lost and confused. The result is that we give more power to the force of fear. Unconsciously, we ensure that fear keeps us in its grip.

Naming Fear

In today's workplace, fear is ever-present. In some workplaces, it is palpable. Job layoffs or plant closings are examples of direct causes. In other workplaces, it is much more discreet, hovering in the background. Fear can be created by less obvious but equally threatening means, such as managers withholding praise, giving unjust performance evaluations, or suddenly adding responsibilities to the job description without giving counterbalancing authority or resources.

Fear attacks self-esteem and self-confidence, either directly or indirectly. Over time, undefined or unspoken fear wearies and paralyzes. How can workers function in such an atmosphere? They make accommodations and adjustments to protect themselves. They do not speak up at meetings. They do not challenge authority even if they are sure that the decision being made is wrong. They do not make suggestions or take the lead. They avoid drawing attention to themselves. They do not take risks because to do so might introduce conflict or other unintended consequences.

Facing reality is the only effective way to deal with fear. We must bring ourselves to look at the unknown. We must ask ourselves whether our fear is based in reality or imagination. We must find ways to lessen its power over us, and find an inner truth to which we can anchor our souls.

Where do we learn coping skills? For some, the source is family and friends. For others, it may be guidance of religious leaders or health care professionals. But whatever the source, the individual must come to an understanding of what is truly meaningful and of value in life.

Facing Fear

How can one begin to face fear? The first, essential step is to understand and accept one's own values and beliefs as valid and true. From there, the adapting skill must be built step by step. Philanthropist Sir John Templeton has devised a practical approach, as seen below, that can be useful as a starting point.

I suggest that when you are in a fearful place, you put yourself in the company of survivors you respect and admire. Observe how they live and think and act. Talk to them. Allow yourself to be vulnerable. Risk being written off as a coward or a failure by asking for help. Ask them to tell you their stories. Ask them how they found the courage to deal with their fears. Ask them how they found the determination to go on despite the pain and confusion and sorrow. Ask them how they found the light at the end of the tunnel and how the experience shaped their lives. Nourish and warm yourself in the comfort and wisdom they have to offer.

When you are in a place of fear, avoid the company of people who are inflexible and judgmental. Try not to admonish yourself or expect yourself to simply carry on as usual. Don't ignore fear or pretend it does not exist. Fear is real. Don't let yourself be trapped in an environment that feeds your feelings of isolation and forces you to carry the crushing weight of other people's expectations.

Defining Fear
How to Blast Fear from Your Life

"Any scientist can tell you that the proper definition of any problem is the biggest single step toward its solution," says philanthropist Sir John Templeton in *Worldwide Laws of Life: 200 Eternal Spiritual Principles.* "A lot of people are living in the abject depressive atmosphere of the darkness of fear."

Sir John suggests preparing a personal launchpad from which to blast off from anxieties, worries and fears. The launchpad is a detailed list of everything that is disturbing, worrying or causing concern. He suggests beginning by using several categories: fear of the unknown, fear of bodily harm, fear of failure, fear of being unloved, fear of being ridiculed and special personal fears.

The next step is to examine the fears one by one, asking where the fear originated and waiting for an answer from the deep recesses of your mind. Gradually, he says, you will increase your understanding. That, combined with knowledge, experience, positive mental attitude, love and prayer, will free you from fear forever.

Source: Templeton, Sir John. *Worldwide Laws of Life: 200 Eternal Spiritual Principles*. Radnor, Pennsylvania: Templeton Foundation Press, 1997. Adapted from "Living the Law," pages 55, 57 & 58.

Look at your own fear. Ask yourself what it is that you really fear. Is it a concrete dread? Loss of your job? Loss of security in knowing where you stand in the working world? Loss of a promotion? Lack of respect from your peers? Embarrassment at being exposed as weak because you are driven to admit you need help?

Or are they deep-in-the-soul fears? Not being in control? Not knowing what tomorrow will bring? Not being loved? Not being loving? Not feeling worthy of love or capable of loving?

Dealing with concrete fears is easier. It is possible to develop managing skills. It means asking "What is the worst that can happen?" and answering honestly, and making plans. It means visualizing the fear and deciding what you can do if the fear materializes. Whether one ever needs to take action at all is another question. The fear may *never* materialize. If it does, it may not be in the dreadful form previously imagined. The point is to give oneself the comfort of knowing that one need not necessarily live without hope. One need not live with feelings of helplessness. One need not regard oneself as living at the mercy of circumstances.

To deal with the deep-in-the-soul fears is more difficult. But dealing with them is the ultimate reality. With a true and abiding sense of one's spiritual core, one will be blessed with the strength to withstand everything and come out changed but whole.

Two common concrete fears are losing one's financial independence and losing one's health. For those who have faced imminent death, nothing can come close to being as fundamentally shattering—not even fear of destitution in old age. (That's why I describe my experience as a gift.)

I am not suggesting that a dread-filled moment of truth is an inoculation against fear. I am suggesting that absolute truthfulness is what brings the courage and strength to live life wholly.

The Fierceness of Truth

Telling the truth is a demanding, challenging act. Few are able to accept unvarnished truth without shielding their minds and hearts. Whether it is the truth we perceive about ourselves or the truth we perceive about our circumstances, it can be extremely uncomfortable. Why? Because truthfulness is fearless. It cannot be denied. It demands change. It requires response.

In the workplace context, truth is a commodity that can be as troublesome as it is essential.

Imagine this: You believe absolutely in respect for the individual. That, for you, is a bedrock value on which you accept no compromise.

But what if you are being subjected to sexual harassment or racial taunts? You refuse to accept this treatment and you regard it as your duty to report immediately. But by reporting it, you are putting your superiors on the line. They must face the issue. But they do not want to deal with it because the person you are accusing is powerful and important. In the fierceness of your truth, you are fearless. You demand action. Your fierceness is just as unwelcomed as the truth you feel compelled to tell. The result is intense discomfort because you are bringing others face-to-face with their fears for themselves.

The very declaration of your truth brings you strength and courage. If you deny your truth, you will find yourself sitting on a volcano. You will never be sure if and when it may explode. You will always be anxious. You will never be safe within yourself unless you name the fear and take the irrevocable step of telling your truth wherever it needs to be told. Naming the fear and declaring the truth lift the anxiety.

The same is true for your superiors. If they turn away, if they shield their minds and hearts, if they practice denial, they will find themselves sitting on their own volcanoes. There will be no peace in their souls ever again. But if they acknowledge their responsibility and react with compassion, they will be blessed with the strength and courage they need to face the fear, deal with it and set it aside.

You have to decide as an individual whether you want to know and whether you are willing to make the commitment to deal with whatever your truth brings. You have to decide whether you are willing to enter reality as a complete participant or give up control by moving away from it. You have to understand that if you refuse to deal with reality, you are giving the fear of the unknown power over you. You have to understand that you cannot expect guarantees. The unknown exists and it is not reasonable to expect anyone or anything—your life partner or your employer—to be responsible for managing the disagreeable or difficult experiences that reality can bring.

At the same time, it *is* reasonable to expect that you should not be required to live or work in a fearful or dishonest place. You have a right to expect integrity and authenticity. In the workplace, that means you cannot expect your employer to guarantee you a job for life or even working conditions that are unchanging and always comfortable. But you can expect that every effort will be made to ensure fair treatment and honest communication.

Positive Fear

Some people claim that fear is a great motivator—in fact, the most effective motivator. They say that fear makes people responsive and innovative. They point to emergency workers who swing into action when disaster strikes. Crisis counselors, ambulance attendants and firefighters, for example, work under enormous stress. They deal with fear as a fact of life—the fear of those they are expected to rescue and their own fear of making a mistake that could cost a life, perhaps even their own.

It is true that some people do their best work under fire. For them the adrenaline rush is what enables them to rise to extraordinary challenges. The nature of the fear may not be life-threatening, but it is fear all the same. Any entrepreneur will tell you that fear is often a daily driver that can push one to excellence.

So, it is possible to use fear in a constructive, positive way. People who are able to do that rob fear of its negative power. They accept fear as a part of life and accustom themselves to living on a roller coaster that rockets from periods of calm to periods of gut-wrenching fear. The lows are wretched, but the highs are fantastic. They thrive on the exhilaration and cannot imagine living any other way.

But this approach to fear, while useful, is not a strategy that can be maintained indefinitely. Lifesavers commonly burn out from stress. Even entrepreneurs who do not hold human lives in their hands burn out from the intensity of the effort.

Enabling Fear

Generally, fear is not a positive force for most people in today's workplace. For them there is no exhilaration because they have precious little control of the roller coaster. For them, the highs and lows are imposed by external forces. Their fear is much more insidious, mundane and life-sapping because they cannot assure themselves of success at the end of the crisis. In fact, there may not *be* a crisis. They are not trained to assess risks and take action. The option of independent action may well be closed to them. Their fear is more often left to fester, eating away at them and gradually debilitating their spirits.

One would think that any reasonable, thinking human being would choose to escape fear. Actually, the opposite is common. Festering fear can become a familiar companion. It can be used as a way to explain or deny inadequacies, failures or resistance to change. It can be comforting in its way because it allows one to refuse to see, understand or deal with demands one feels unable to meet.

The price fear-deniers pay is significant. Pretending fear doesn't exist takes tremendous energy. Lying to oneself consistently can be difficult. Flexibility and creativity are frozen. They become too dangerous to let loose, because letting them loose means letting fear out of the cage as well. Any risk, however small, becomes too great.

The very nature of corporations, however well-intentioned and supportive they may be, is to enable the fearful to avoid having to deal with their fear. Corporations make promises: You work. We pay. Everyone gets to be secure and comfortable. No one ever need worry again.

Corporations present themselves as the embodiment of a safe and secure future. They have to do that in order to attract the workers they need. But everyone knows, if they allow themselves to look into their hearts and minds, that corporations cannot be the embodiment of safety and security. Ways of doing business are changing. Global market dynamics are forcing mergers, acquisitions, redeployment of resources and shifting priorities and plans. No corporation can truly cocoon and protect.

And yet for corporations to survive, they must persuade their employees to turn a blind eye to the fragility of the cocoon. They must make every effort to avoid talking about, thinking about or even recognizing fear. No one can afford to admit that the corporation can be ripped apart or destroyed without warning.

For employees, facing workplace fear means recognizing that the cocoon is fragile and vulnerable. It means it is not perfect and may not last beyond tomorrow. It means accepting that one day they may be forced to leave the cocoon and take responsibility for their own future. There is no magic wand that can hold change at bay. The spell can be broken at any time.

In the 1950s, substance, assurance and comfort were promises that could largely be kept. The language of corporations was clear and unequivocal. But in the 1980s, this started to change. Today, corporations still talk about themselves as places of substance, but they also talk about being flexible and entrepreneurial. It is not good enough anymore for employees to be just good at their work. Now, corporations want more than loyalty and total commitment.

So, what are employees to believe? Whom can they trust? On what can they rely? As they try to deal with these contradictory messages and hang on to their jobs, they want to believe in the substance they convinced themselves exists. But more and more they are forced to realize that there is nothing standing between their current circumstances and no job at all, other than their own health and ability to survive.

Enlightening Fear

What I see as the big development in the living workplace of the 21st century is a massive mind shift in the ranks of corporate workers. They are going to wake up to the realization that the corporate cocoon is a fragile thing. In the end, the cocoon does not have the substance they talked themselves into believing was there. Some workers are now understanding that security and safety within the corporation are more imaginary than real. A few are realizing that they misplaced their hopes and dreams when they put their trust in the corporation.

Will there be a mass exodus of workers from corporations all over the world? Will every employee reinvent himself or herself as an entrepreneur? No, because not everyone can tolerate risk; not everyone is able to live with the prospect of waking up every morning and wondering when the next job is going to come through the door.

What will happen is that fear—debilitating, degrading fear—will give way to clarity, determination and excitement. Workers will allow themselves to face their fears and will refuse to allow the force of fear to continue exercising its power. They will create a revolution within the corporation by declaring themselves as individuals with courage—the courage to demand change, to make change, to direct change. They will be the embodiment of what every corporation both craves and fears—creative, innovative, entrepreneurial and empowered.

Today's workers, many of whom have been in the workforce for many years, are already coming to this realization and acting upon it. But the full force will be felt as new workers, many now still in school, move in. They will come from a different starting point with different expectations and different principles. Will they feel fear? Of course. That is part of the human condition. But how they react and respond to it will be different. They will come in looking at the nature of work very differently. Corporations will find themselves pushed to adapt their business models accordingly. If they stick with the same ways of dealing with fear by giving false hope and using ephemeral power to maintain control, they will be the losers.

In fact, one of the biggest battlegrounds will be over the issue of control. Corporations say that they want their employees to be entrepreneurial, but the nature of the entrepreneur is to exercise a degree of control. The entrepreneur says, "I am going to do something about this. It may not be much and it may not help, but I am going to try it anyway because it is in my nature."

In the corporate model, the current attitude is to urge employees to be proactive, but at the same time to stay within tightly prescribed limits. "Be entrepreneurial," employees are told, "but do not proceed until you have the approval of all appropriate levels of management." The control, and the expectation of the right to exercise control, is still very much in the hands of employers.

In the latter part of the 20th century, employees who chafed against this degree of control generally took themselves out of the corporation and made places or found places where they could be more independent and entrepreneurial. In the 21st century, incoming workers will decide much more quickly. "Move it or lose us," they will say to employers. They will not have the patience or the willingness to listen to employers telling them that they must stay within strictly defined parameters. They will not be willing to wait five years to see how things work out, or to take the prospect of job security and a pension when they retire as sufficient or appropriate compensation for giving up their sense of independence and power.

The Truth About Work

Stripped to its core, the naked truth about work in the living workplace of the 21st century is that workers will not tolerate working with fear. I suggest that as workers develop a concentrated sense of their own souls and spirits, they will come to a vision of work that frees them from the chains of fear. They will discover ways to name and address their fears, view the unknown and come to terms with uncertainty. They will find and exercise courage and strength of spirit. As they do so, they will change the very nature of work and the workplace.

The new workers will not suddenly turn *en masse* into fearless creatures who are willing to gamble all. There will be degrees of enlightenment and self-discovery. But as a group, they will recognize and deal with fear. They will begin to live their lives with a degree of clarity beyond the norm of the 20th century. And this clarity will not be something they switch on and off when they cross the corporate threshold. They will bring this clarity to all parts of their lives. Once an individual has met fear and found a way to go forward, there is no turning back. There is no longer refuge to be found in denial or superficiality.

If one chooses to look, it is easy to see this every day as workers move through a transition period already in progress. The upheaval inherent in layoffs, mergers and reorganizations is upsetting and challenging, and very difficult to survive without a strong emotional support system. Human resources directors who are versed in, or prepared to talk about, transition and fear are few and far between. They are only just beginning to find a new language for dealing with transition and fear.

Many workers seek compromise as a way to deal with fear, but it is an effort doomed to failure. I do not believe there can be a middle ground between denying fear and facing fear. It is like cracks in a dam: once they start to appear, the end is inevitable. One can ignore the cracks and be swept away by the deluge when the dam breaks apart. But as soon as one admits that the cracks exist, there is no going back to a state of not knowing. One must understand what the cracks mean and the dangers they represent. It is possible to paper over the cracks in the hope that the dam will hold a little bit longer—maybe just long enough to find the dry, safe ground of another job or early retirement. But the knowledge is there and the fear is there, and both must be faced.

The cost of trying to find that compromise between denying fear and facing fear is significant. The Business and Economic Round-table on Mental Health, a volunteer organization of senior business executives and health professionals concerned with mental health issues, estimates that dealing with depression alone in the workplace costs the Canadian and U.S. economies (U.S.) $60 billion annually.[23]

Recently, *Fast Company* reported that job stress is estimated to cost U.S. industry $200 billion to $300 billion annually in absenteeism, diminished productivity, employee turnover, accidents, workers' compensation, and direct medical, legal and insurance fees.[24]

For workers, the price is paralyzing creative and intuitive abilities or showing symptoms of emotional and physical illness. Individuals also pay a price in their personal lives. No matter how hard they try to walk away at the end of the workday, the anxiety will seep into and affect every other part of life.

"What happens if I try to build a life dedicated to avoiding all danger and unnecessary risk?" asks Sam Keen, author of *Learning to Fly* and *Fire in the Belly*. "If 'security' and 'safety' become watchwords by which I live, gradually the circle of my experience becomes small and claustrophobic. I need to live near the vital edge between fear and fascination to help me remember that, so long as I live, I will tremble and wonder."[25]

I am convinced that as workers connect with their souls and their truths, they will change the way they work. Workers will devise new personal models that acknowledge their hearts. In my view, the intense desire for heartfelt work is going to be one of the key factors driving the way the workplace will change in the 21st century.

The path to security and safety lies in realizing that it is possible to face fear step by step. Fear exists in all of us. The only effective counterbalance to fear is the amount of truth we have in our lives and our souls. The more truth we have in our lives, the easier it becomes to deal with fear. But truth—brilliant, shining, answering, comforting, guiding truth—is not something that usually comes in a blinding, miraculous flash. Finding the truth within us is a gradual process. So too is finding the courage and strength to face the fear within us.

"Go put your creed into
  your deed,
"Nor speak with double
  tongue."

Ralph Waldo Emerson
(1803–1882),
Ode, Concord (July 4,
1857), Stanza 5

CHAPTER 6

Say, Listen, Hear

C ommunication dictates much of the nature of workplace relationships. It can be used to create and maintain distance, or to
link and bond. But workers are becoming distrustful of and impa-
tient with the keep-your-place attitude and directive language still
common in the corporate world.

In the 21st-century workplace, workers will demand a new
language, one they are already discovering for themselves and using
in their private lives. They are already seeking truthful communication as well as passion, integrity and clarity. They want a business
model and content more expressive of the way in which they see
themselves connecting to the workplace.

As Oliver Wendell Holmes said, "One's mind, once stretched by
a new idea, never regains its original dimensions." This new, living

language will grow with the e-lance economy. Total trust, sharing and openness in communications will become the new standard, essential, in fact, for corporate survival in the living workplace of the 21st century.

The Tyranny of Technology

During the last decade of the 20th century, corporations leapt enthusiastically on the communications bandwagon. They brewed a fine concoction of direct, easily accessible information and splashed it over employees and customers alike. They added intranets, Web sites, video streaming and satellite news conferences to the established stars of the marketing firmament—billboards, bulletin boards, newsletters, toll-free telephone lines, group e-mails, brochures, advertising supplements, open forums with senior management, and annual reports with impressive-sounding accounts of corporate contributions to the community.

Technology made it possible to develop this integrated, multipronged, fast-reaction-time approach and to take advantage of a fantastic opportunity to reach diverse, widely spread audiences with consistent, well-crafted, up-to-the-minute messages. Marrying the marvels of technology to central command was brilliantly successful.

For all that, the content, tone and approach often did not change. Terms such as *sharing, caring, service* and *commitment* were used with casual ease, even as corporations slashed workforces, increased the use of voice-mail, insisted everyone had to do more with less, and walked the talk of increasing shareholder value. As corporations discovered that no one need be left out of the communications loop, they were also able to tighten their hold on content and distribution. At the same time, they slimmed down the message to sound bites and bland statements that implied much, but said little.

Face-to-Face Communication

In a sense, technology is a great leveler. It permits everyone to take part in the conversation. But it is also a distancer because it removes the opportunity to read the subtle signs and messages that come from looking into someone's eyes, hearing their tone of voice and reading their body language. As John Galsworthy said in *Flowering Wilderness*, "One's eyes are what one is, one's mouth is what one becomes." It is virtually impossible to look into somebody's eyes and not develop a sense of whether you are in a trusting, truthful relationship, regardless of the words being spoken. Workers accustomed to direct, personal contact rely on their discerning and intuitive skills, and treasure the gift face-to-face conversations bring.

The distancing impact of technology has been emphasized by the focus on form rather than content. Downgrading of discernment and intuition has also had an effect. For established corporate workers, the byproducts of the disruption of person-to-person contact and relationships are often discomfort, dissatisfaction and distrust.

For new workers, who have been using technology as a linking and communication agent since they were in diapers, the effect is different. They are so at ease with technology, they have no sense of discomfort or dissatisfaction. For them, e-mail and Internet chat rooms are givens.

As a result, for the time being, the distancing impact of technology is of lesser concern. But in the long term, the distancing effect will become a critical issue. Discernment and intuition are still important, but they cannot be used fully when technology is the dominant interface. Face-to-face communication is necessary to link imagining and creating. Workers must be accustomed to or in the habit of face-to-face interaction if they are to make the leap from well-trained technicians to leading-edge communicators.

As the authors of *The Cluetrain Manifesto: The End of Business as Usual* say, "Corporate firewalls have kept smart employees in and smart markets out. It's going to cause real pain to tear those walls down. But the result will be a new kind of conversation. And it will be the most exciting conversation business has ever engaged in."[26]

The Art of Communication

When we hear the word *communication*, we often think only of the saying, or telling, probably because we are so used to being "told" things that don't necessarily interest us. We get so used to the daily assaults by radio, television, telephone, billboards and electronic signs, we lose the habit of really listening and hearing.

Listening is the physical act of giving attention. Hearing describes both the physical act of listening *and* the intellectual and emotional acts of absorbing and learning. True communication encompasses speaking, listening and hearing. Communication without all three elements is by definition stunted and incomplete.

It is the exceptional corporation indeed that would suggest its communications' posture is not direct and honest. I believe the corporate intent is sincere. The chasm between intent and result is deep, however, and it is being dug deeper as corporations rely more on the tools of technology and less on human interaction. In the pell-mell rush toward e-communication, e-commerce and the e-lance economy, the underlying assumption seems to be that technology is the solution rather than the enabler, and that speed equals quality. The saying, or telling, is there, but the crucial elements of listening and hearing are lost in the process.

This loss will become a striking feature of the 21st-century workplace, as new workers enter. Often, they are more conversant with computers than with people. But their social skills are less well developed. They are handicapped from the outset because they are generally ill-at-ease or unpracticed in terms of face-to-face speaking, listening and hearing.

There is a reason why brainstorming has been around for so long. It works. That's why running brainstorming sessions is one of the great joys in my work today. The foundation for creative break-throughs is built on articulating ideas, listening to others, absorbing what they have said, framing responses. It often means building on something one may have intuitively comprehended but not really understood until hearing it spoken by someone else or hearing oneself say it out loud. When the say–listen–hear circle of communication is broken, the potentially wonderful and inventive nature of the human mind is greatly circumscribed.

Hard Edges, Soft Skills

Technological advances have indeed been a fantastic boon to business in terms of speed and scope. Time has been compressed into femtoseconds. Geography is irrelevant. But what corporations—and the people who work in them—sometimes forget is that what makes a message important is the content, not the means of sending it.

As Mark Starowicz, project director and executive director of the Canadian Broadcasting Corporation's "The Canadian History Project," said, "What we are seeing may be occasioned by one piece of technology—the microchip—but it is not one revolution; it is a cluster of revolutions. Sometimes—I find this interesting—we are actually seeing the return of old media that we thought were dead or static. The digital age has, for example, resurrected telegraphy in the form of e-mail, restoring an almost Victorian level of letter-writing. It is a revolution in telephony, a century-old medium where we weren't expecting much excitement."[27]

When workers send e-mails, they are sending letters, reports, proposals or responses. When they leave voice-mail messages, they are exchanging notes of information. Yet the prevailing view is to downgrade the need to learn how to develop and present thoughtful, well-crafted, clear content. The definition of technological literacy rarely, if ever, appears to include writing and speaking skills.

When workers use real-time video, video conferencing and other highly sophisticated technological tools, they are still sitting in isolation in front of a monitor. Even if they can see the person with whom they are linked, they will be blocked by a barrier that does not let them see or hear, for example, a foot tapping impatiently. Nor will they have the opportunity to build a friendship bit by bit by sharing moments of understanding over an informal lunch.

The day will come when 21st-century workers finally begin to understand that they need and want something more. The tools, however sophisticated, will lose their luster, as workers realize they are not truly connecting to their workplaces or to each other. That is when the demand for a new language characterized by honesty, energy and clarity will become a clamor—the day workers become aware of their hunger for true, full circle, say–listen–hear communication. They will be as hungry for it as they are for respect, regard and a spiritually supportive workplace.

This realization will also dawn on employers as they wage the war for talent. The first effects in the marketplace of knowledge workers being fought over are already being felt. But the shortcomings of these workers are also becoming apparent. As reported in *Stepping Up: Skills and Opportunities in the Knowledge Economy*, a study done in 2000 by the Conference Board of Canada, these workers are technically skilled but they generally do not have the "soft" skills, such as teamwork and oral and written communications. They are valuable for their technical talents and skill for moving messages across time and space. But they have not developed the discerning and intuitive skills of human discourse. They are not equipped to say, listen and hear beyond tightly defined boundaries. They are clumsy in social environments. These workers will become liabilities that corporations cannot tolerate if they are to compete successfully in the global marketplace.

Joseph F. Coates, president of Coates & Jarratt, Inc., a Washington, D.C. company engaged in futures research, lays some of the responsibility at the door of the educational system. "The most important skills for the worker that are largely eluding the educational structure today are skills in communication—not just reading and writing, but in computation, and perhaps most importantly of all, in listening. Other skill needs will emphasize human interaction, sensitivity to people, ability to work in teams—the sorts of things that are reflected in a number of interesting books and reports on 'emotional intelligence.'"

Consider the Source

The World Wide Web has flung open the doors to goods, services and information. On the positive side, with an Internet connection and a few clicks, it is possible to find a date, get information about the environment, locate statistical data, join a chat room, and buy things you never knew existed. There is no question that it is a powerful, extremely valuable tool.

But how credible is the information? How can you identify and judge the authenticity and credentials of the source? How can you discern the truth of what you are being told? How can you verify it? In the past, you had a fighting chance of finding someone you knew who could give you that assurance. You could walk down the street to the store or office and confirm that the business exists. You could double-check by comparison shopping in your community or calling the local equivalent of the Better Business Bureau.

So, we find ourselves in a technological dilemma. We can find anything we need to know or want to have quickly without having to be concerned about where in the world it may be. But the nature of the tool works against our need to evaluate the credibility of the source. We are constrained in using our discerning and intuitive skills to make reasonably informed judgments.

This realization is already surfacing. As people are misinformed, manipulated and cheated, they become angry and suspicious. They will start looking for concrete evidence of credibility.

For corporations doing business anywhere, it will be imperative to recognize that truth in communication is going to be regarded as the line in the sand. Workers and consumers alike are going to insist on truth. They will react against communications designed to convince, manipulate, guide or maneuver. Honesty, integrity and verification are going to assume highly visible and critical roles.

The driving force will be understanding that technology is a magnificent tool—but it is only a tool and it cannot do everything. It takes human intelligence and knowledge to drive the tool, make it, use it and shape it. It is not something mystical or otherworldly that has descended miraculously from the ether. It is a people-driven invention that, however revolutionary, is still just a construction— not a living force.

Causing Effects

Is it possible that the next generation of workers, having already embraced technology as a way of life, will decide they can live without human relationships and daily face-to-face contact? One should consider the implications. If they lose—or never learn—the habit of personal communication and the value of talking face-to-face, what will be the effect on the workplace and workers' lives?

One effect will be to change and reduce the number of workers needed. Because workers will see themselves, and be encouraged to see themselves, as data-inputters or information-exchangers, they will no longer concern themselves with how information or ideas are created or used. They will become highly efficient masters of the technology and totally disengaged from thought. They will have no need to communicate beyond minimal essentials. Participation in true communication will be the province of a select, powerful few.

For these new workers, the concept of a new workplace language will be one of limited engagement and clear direction. "Tell me what you want me to do, give me the technology and leave me alone. Do not expect me to become involved. I am not interested. I live my real life somewhere else."

Another effect will be on the forms of language between workers, and between employers and employees. Just as the business suit is giving way to casual wear, casual language will replace formal language. Small courtesies and social graces are already disappearing. Who needs to bother acknowledging e-mails or returning calls? It is temptingly easy to hit delete. Besides, who has time to do anything but the absolutely essential?

A third effect will be a scattering of the workplace in physical terms and a disintegration of the workplace in emotional terms. This is already happening. People work on the move from virtual offices or from home-based offices, keeping in touch by e-mail. To the dot.com generation, already accustomed to digital mobility, this will be a natural choice. Employers will opt for it because it is cost-efficient and also removes complicated human contact and problems that can be so disruptive to the business day. But the net result will be a loss of control over employees who are not only accustomed to instant gratification, but also not able or willing to listen to or hear anything that does not directly affect them. They will have no interest in the bigger picture. All they will want to know is what it means to them personally, right now. Employers will find themselves at the mercy of employees who are largely unknown quantities, impervious to the usual blandishments, and ready to change jobs at a moment's notice because there is no emotional tie to the current employer or corporation. They will have disconnected without ever having connected.

Reinventing Communication

Even if the dot.com generation disconnects without ever having connected, eventually, as they mature, they will find themselves seeking interpersonal relationships in the workplace. Dr. Axel Zweck, head of the Future Technologies Division at the Association of German Engineers, describes it as "fundamental human needs concerning direct personal contacts and face-to-face communications."

Employers who opt out, who allow the bricks and mortar to crumble and who lose the habit of face-to-face discussions, will pay the price in diminished control, trust and authenticity. Employers who reinvent communication by acknowledging that content counts more than form and by recognizing that technology is a tool rather than an end in itself will succeed in riding the *tsunami* the dot.com workers bring.

The new workers will be looking for content, authenticity, truthfulness and trust. Just as they reject dress codes, standard working hours, and working at a central site, they will also reject old patterns of communication. The communications model will have to change to accommodate these demands. Control and manipulation will have to give way to trust and truth.

In *The Heart Aroused: Poetry and the Preservation of the Soul in Corporate America*, David Whyte encourages the courageous spirit, finding voice and using sound. He goes on to say, "The voice is as important to our identity as anything we possess. We ask ourselves if we really have *a voice* in this organization, want reassurance that we can *give voice* to our opinions, and if we cannot, speak *sotto voce* to those few in whom we choose to confide."

In today's workplace, speech and language are directly linked to performance, compliance, fear, need and acceptance. Many corporate managers use their voices, words and body language to coerce and control. What must change in the living workplace is how managers use language. They must understand that language inspires and motivates on subtle as well as more obvious levels. They must expand their understanding of language in the context of the growing diversity of the workplace.

Gifted orators have always understood the power of voice in the sense of physical manifestations—measured delivery, dramatic pauses, subtle gestures, an air of sincerity. Their real feelings may not have any relationship to their message, but the message will be delivered compellingly and convincingly.

In today's workplace, it is not difficult to observe the effects of chaos and fear. Voice pitch rises, words start tumbling out, hands tremble, sweat glistens on the forehead . . . clearly, stress levels are rising.

What both employers and employees need to do is become aware of and sensitive to the voices around them and alert to the gestures that accompany the sounds. Voices and body language tell as much about the authenticity of the message as do the words. Do the actions match the words? Good speakers have a natural advantage, but it does not guarantee effectiveness.

Some years ago, I watched a writer of a motivational book series deliver a powerful pitch to a mixed audience of loyal readers. At one point, he asked someone in the audience to lend him a copy of the book. A young woman gave him her copy. It was clear from the way she handled it that she treasured it. He flipped it open, made his point, slammed it shut and *threw* it back to her. She looked devastated. At that moment, I realized the audience meant nothing to him as people and that the books were nothing more to him than a money-earning commodity. His actions belied the authenticity of his words.

Workers and managers also need to both separate and integrate the words and the actions. An accomplished speaker can weave a spell. But if you take the text and read it without the sound of the voice, the inflections and the drama, you can concentrate in a different way on what the words mean. You may find subtleties or clarity that otherwise would have escaped you.

The question of voice in terms of physical sound is fundamental. There are many different voices: cooperative, challenging, compassionate, caring, concerned, noncommittal, questioning, collaborative, aggressive, assertive, intimidating. The challenge for everyone in the workplace is to find a way to convey voice in a world where more and more is communicated by e-mail. Writing clipped sentences, dropping salutations or skipping connectors between thoughts or statements all contribute to a tone that may be perceived as aggressive, challenging, intimidating or uncaring. The news may be wonderful and the intentions friendly, but in the absence of voice and in the presence of clumsy writing the message will at best be mangled—and at worst misunderstood.

In environments where fear is rampant, truth and clarity are extremely difficult to maintain. Clumsy writing combined with the absence of physical voice or with the presence of contradictory body language will ensure that the fear spreads like a contagious disease. For employers in particular, this will present a challenge as they reinvent their corporate communications.

The physical voice is an instrument that permits the speaker to touch another's soul. If we also speak with passion, clarity and truth, we increase our chances of being listened to and heard. But if we start from the position of getting or maintaining control, the intent to manipulate will come through in the tone.

If the CEO starts from a position of truth, does the best possible job of presenting the case, and asks for support, he or she surrenders control of the outcome. This is the most effective approach because it is regarding, collaborative and honest. It is far more likely to succeed, especially over the long term.

The Living Language

How can this new, living language come into its own in a technological age where workers send e-mails to colleagues in the next cubicle, as well as around the block or across the world? Aren't we being distanced and impeded from developing relationships of trust and regard, by working at arm's length through e-mail where everything is so speeded up there is no room for caring?

Distancing technology isn't the only barrier between workers and the new language. Another barrier is the pain and grief some people may carry with them through life and which affects how they communicate with others. This is something with which each individual must deal. As David Whyte says (in *The Heart Aroused*), "Inhabiting the full body, the long body, as many North American Native traditions say, with the voice, may be one of the great soul challenges of adult life." The voice that Whyte speaks of is the living language.

Yet the new, living language will come into its own in the 21st century because the new worker will demand it. In fact, the new worker will be hungry for any language, but will resist what he or she perceives as the language of older generations. The words will have to be different from the words used with older workers, but the foundation on which they are based will be the same. Personal contact, face-to-face conversation, seeing and hearing voice in order to listen, hear, absorb and understand will all be required.

This need for personal contact in order to build trust will have the ironic effect of shrinking individuals' worlds. On one hand, workers will have the means to work without regard for geographical limits. On the other, they will find themselves tending toward working with people in the next office or down the block. Being in closer touch will come more and more to mean having the option to be in personal, physical contact.

The Impact on the Soul

Technology is presented as freeing; in fact, it can just as easily become a form of bondage because there is no escape from the virtual office. The 24-hour day, 7-day week becomes the norm very quickly. The impact on the soul of workers is already profound.

I think the acceptance of technology as an end in itself is anesthetizing the soul. As the song says, just keep dancing because if we keep moving, it must mean we are getting somewhere. Voices become muted, physically and in content. Courageous speech disappears. Feelings are pushed down and out of sight.

Those who have the courage to resist, who maintain their voices and exercise their communications skills, are empowered by personal strength. They are nourished by honesty and openness, and they reject control and manipulation. They are the ones most likely to lead the dot.com generation to the new language.

Who, What, How

Harry S. Truman, the 33rd president of the United States, said, "If you can't convince them, confuse them." To me this demonstrates the demeaning superficiality of the outdated business model that was so long accepted as the norm in the 20th-century corporate world.

Writer and author Stuart Crainer says,

> "The art of communication has always lain at the heart of effective management. On that all are agreed. But the question is, communication with whom? Traditionally, managers were more willing to talk to each other but regarded as demeaning to talk to humble employees. The man operating the machine doffed his cap to management or raised a finger as managers made their way to elevated offices. Times change. Now the job of management is to communicate with everyone, shareholders, the media, colleagues, superiors, customers, suppliers and even the people doing the work on the factory floor. The measure of managers in the late 20th century is how well they communicate, not so much what they communicate."[28]

The *Harvard Business Review on Change* sets out in precise detail its recommendations for the "how" of communication. "In more successful transformation efforts, executives use all existing communication channels to broadcast the vision. They turn boring and unread company newsletters into lively articles about the vision. They take ritualistic and tedious quarterly management meetings and turn them into exciting discussions of the transformation. They throw out much of the company's generic management education and replace it with courses that focus on business problems and the new vision. The guiding principle is simple: Use every possible channel, especially those that are being wasted on nonessential information."[29]

In my opinion, managers' ability to communicate in the 21st century is going to be measured by both the "what" and the "how." They will be of absolutely equal value. Emphasizing "how" over "what" reeks of manipulation. Workers are going to demand truth. Honest communication will be the only acceptable response. Trying to confuse workers will backfire because instead of continuing to accept it even though they do not understand it, they will turn away in disbelief and distrust. Some are bound to leave the company altogether.

For the "how," I recommend publisher Joseph Pulitzer's advice: "Put it before them briefly so that they will read it, clearly so they will appreciate it, picturesquely so they will remember it, and, above all, accurately so that they will be guided by its light."

The New Standard

It is very difficult to communicate the truth validly and in its entirety. It is equally difficult to communicate the true value of work and the true value of soul in the workplace. What will constitute the standard of the new, living language?

The foundation for understanding, developing and recognizing the new standard of communication is equal responsibility and accountability. As Dr. Samuel Johnson said three centuries ago, "In order that all men may be taught to speak truth, it is necessary that all likewise should learn to hear it." The onus is on corporations to speak continually with truth and integrity. The onus is on employees to recognize and respond with equal truth and integrity. As Dr. Johnson also said, "Integrity without knowledge is weak and useless, and knowledge without integrity is dangerous and dreadful."

It is unreasonable for employees to expect employers to set in motion the quest for the new standard if they are not willing to accept responsibility for collaboration. If employees divide the corporate world into "us" and "them," if they do not understand the connectedness, if they do not honestly create and present what they truly care about and want to achieve, then achieving anything remotely like the new standard will be impossible.

Communication, like truth, has many levels. It is naive for anyone to sit back and suggest that such a complex interaction can be managed and maintained without everyone playing a role. It is also naive and dishonest to listen to what is presented as the corporate truth and then simply respond by saying, "Well, that is not my truth, therefore, I will not pay attention to it or accept its validity." It is not enough to rely on the communications or human resources professionals to deliver the message. Everybody within the corporate structure must also be ready to listen, hear and contribute.

One of the barriers over which both employers and employees must reach is the increasing diversity of the workforce, which is being accentuated by migrating populations and the demands of the global marketplace. As Joseph F. Coates says, "The handwriting is on the wall—diversity is the hallmark of the workplace of the future." By 2033, he says, ethnic minorities may account for 30 percent of the total population of the United States.[30]

Cultural imperatives change the way in which people communicate and understand. All parties must be prepared to adjust with goodwill. Dr. Lionel Laroche, president of ITAP Canada, a consulting company specializing in cultural diversity in the workplace, illustrates this with an example that compares American and Japanese styles of presentation. The Japanese approach is to explain in extremely precise and thorough detail each and every possible option. The goal is to prove that the right conclusion is the only course to pursue. The right conclusion is the last one to be presented. Their presentations are accompanied by numerous charts and plenty of statistics because that is what their audiences expect and require.

The American approach is different. The goal is to give a convincing pitch for the option of choice. Americans begin with the right conclusion and focus on it almost exclusively. Their presentations are distinguished by overviews and summaries of the evidence, with only passing references to other, less desirable options. Their audiences are unwilling to sit still for lengthy dissertations on everything that may be considered. They want to hear what they should consider and why.

If you provide a Japanese-style presentation to an American audience or vice versa, both audiences will be frustrated—one will not be getting enough information and the other will be getting too much. Somehow, contemporary communicators have to find a middle ground. All parties share the responsibility to find it.

Dr. Laroche also cites an example of the importance of finding a common vocabulary. An engineer by training, he spent several months early in his career working for his employer with a counterpart in Germany. Both were called product engineers, but they wasted weeks before they realized that *product engineer* meant something different in their respective cultural contexts. Dr. Laroche arrived expecting to get into the laboratory and start work immediately. His counterpart, however, never did the work directly; he directed a team of technicians. Finally, the frustration of mismatched expectations drove them to ask each other why they were not doing what each expected the other to do. It was only then that they found a middle ground.

Another barrier related to cultural imperatives is individual differences in temperament and concepts of space. Human beings are territorial creatures who need and expect to be treated with dignity and respect, but how they define dignity and respect are different. For example, in North American workplaces, the open-office concept is common. Sometimes, but not always, there are low dividers. Speaking loudly may be interpreted as an intrusion on someone else's space. Coming right up to the workstation without permission may also be interpreted this way. How people enter each others' physical and emotional spaces requires adjustments to the form of communication because individual definitions of "my space" can be markedly different. A vivid everyday example is to look at how (and whether) people line up at a bus stop or grocery store. Do they stand close enough to touch? Do they leave space between?

Chris Christensen, president of Christensen Associates, Inc., a California-based management consulting company, says, "Language, culture and laws must be continuously accommodated by the entire workforce. Intolerance of others' habits and idiosyncrasies will not be tolerated in working relationships."

In the workplace, dignity and respect may be connected to the quality and quantity of information. For example, suppliers may work with corporations frequently and regularly, but how much information are they given? Just enough to do the job, or enough to understand the "why"? When employees receive information by e-mail or voice-mail, the communication enters their private work spaces. Are they addressed as individuals, or are they bombarded with To All Employees circulars?

Job reviews can be another minefield. Is the language and approach directional or absolute? Marilyn Knox, president of Nestlé Canada Inc.'s Nutrition Division, talks about looking at job reviews from the point of view of assessing and managing for employee excellence. She approaches communication in this context from the point of view of integrity, goals, behavior, risk-taking ability and the ability to strengthen others. Assuming an absolute standard and judging performance against it is, in her view, inappropriate and counterproductive because it is not built on a foundation of respect for the individual. In a culturally diverse workplace, however, some employees and managers may be expecting, and be more comfortable with, an absolute review, and uncomfortable with a directional approach. The new standard of communication must understand and accommodate these differences.

If the idea of strengthening the individual, wherever that individual may be placed in the corporation, permeates the corporation and all of its dealings and all of its communications, then that corporation is well on its way to reaching the new standard. Creating and nourishing an environment that honors the individual will result in fiercely strong bonds of loyalty and commitment. As Knox says, "Love lifts you up." Serenity and strength go hand in hand. Weakness and surrender are pushed out of the picture.

Closely related to developing strength is encouraging employees to speak their minds. Demanding agreement and compliance will make day-to-day life seem smoother and more efficient, but in the end will be counterproductive. In the words of Dr. Johnson, "Curiosity is one of the permanent and certain characteristics of a vigorous mind." Vigorous minds, while not always obedient or easy to manage, bring the possibility of initiative, inventiveness and creativity.

Nothing will sabotage efforts to reach the new standard more quickly and effectively than speaking, as Ralph Waldo Emerson said, "with double tongue." As the *Harvard Business Review on Change* says, "Communication comes in both words and deeds and the latter are often the more powerful form. Nothing undermines change more than behavior by important individuals that is inconsistent with their words."[31]

In the end, the focus must be integrity and truth that encompass and acknowledge the values of everyone in the corporation. While their genius is creating profit, leaders today must do more than make money. Their legacy must be creating meaning and compassion that knows no boundaries within a corporate environment.

"Souls are God's jewels,
every one of which is
worth many worlds."

Thomas Traherne,
Centuries
of Meditation

CHAPTER 7

The Spiritual Worker

A s the 20th century ended, the *Encyclopedia of American Religions* identified more than 2,000 religious groups in North America. This is double the number tracked by the publication a mere 20 years before. As well as established religions with roots far back in human history, the *Encyclopedia* lists New Age groups that focus on self-realization, psychology and primacy of the individual.

"Spirituality" has become a catchphrase to describe a broad and deeply felt desire to be connected to something or someone beyond the individual. Many people use the term interchangeably with "ethics," "values" and "morals." Some define *spirituality* as trust. A definition of spirituality I appreciate is "a common understanding that spiritual values are more important than material values and, therefore, a spiritual workplace is one where both employers and employees work together to celebrate and contribute to others."

No matter how spirituality and the spiritual workplace are

defined, however, I feel we have come to a crossroads. Workers want spiritual nourishment. They seek to connect their yearning for the sacred to the ordinary parts of their daily lives.

Is it reasonable to expect an employer to provide spiritual nourishment to employees? What are the consequences for corporations and their employees if the workplace is not spiritually sustaining? What choices are workers making when they realize their workplace environments are not spiritually nourishing?

Soul and Spirit

Spiritual well-being, the very survival of soul, is as critical as physical and emotional well-being on both an individual level and a corporate level.

For me, spirituality is a commitment to faith, expressed in worship, integrity, contribution and celebration. True spirituality creates total peace and harmony because it is integrated into all aspects of life—home, work and community. "Whatever you do, work at it with all your heart, as working for the Lord, not men" (*Colossians 3:23*).

Philanthropist Sir John Templeton defines the spiritual ideal as the "purpose, intent, desire, motivation, incentive and the spirit in which you do anything."[32] Striving for the spiritual ideal will bring peace, commitment and harmony. All will be enriched as a result.

It is not easy, however, to find workplaces that truly honor and enrich the soul or spirit. *Soul* is not a word that is likely to come up at routine management meetings. The struggle to address soul and spirituality in the workplace is apparent in the search for inclusive language that is meaningful to everyone, including those who have given little thought to the matter or those who are unable to articulate it.

Caleb Rosado, PhD, head of the Behavioural Sciences Department at Newbold College in England, defines spirituality as "a state of interconnectedness with the Other—the Divine, the self, the human, the natural—resulting in a state of security with a sense of worthwhile purpose." For him, the key is the concept of attachments, which he defines as the social–spiritual bonds that connect to whatever it is that gives a sense of meaning and purpose to the individual's life.

However defined, "spirituality" is quickly becoming one of the most commonly used words we have today. Clearly, people are seeking a spiritual path or a higher power to help them find and come to terms with the meaning and purpose of life. They have a great hunger for something to sustain them. They desire respect, compassion and concern. What they are seeking is an environment where caring has meaning in terms of individuals being important and caring for others. We all want to be regarded as people who can and do make a difference.

The Search for Spirituality

"The word 'God' is just too close to the chest—literally—for most people in the workplace," says coach and facilitator Michael E. Rock, EdD, because it raises questions of life and death and meaning. Spirituality, however, is more acceptable because it is regarded as generic and inoffensive.

What 21st-century workers describe as spirituality is a desire for a daily life that incorporates ideas of abundance, wisdom, strength, love, faith, imagination, wholeness and health. Like God, these are not words generally heard in every workplace. We hear more about profit and leadership than about wisdom, strength, loyalty and love. We hear more about cynicism and fragmentation than faith and wholeness.

Most religions incorporate the Golden Rule into their belief systems. In its simplest form, the Golden Rule is the principle of treating others as one wishes to be treated. The Dalai Lama expresses it very simply. When I visited India some years ago, I had the honor of meeting him several times. Each visit was memorable, but the moment I recall most vividly was when I asked what he would say to all people, regardless of religious faith. His answer was, "I would tell them just to be a good person because it is very hard to be a good person."

In the spiritual workplace, the meaningful application of this age-old teaching is more far-reaching than simply using team-building exercises to build workplace morale. From the spiritual worker's perspective, team-building exercises based on dignity and honor are important for building mutual respect as well as productivity. They participate more willingly and wholeheartedly if those exercises are placed in a spiritually supportive context.

The Search for Self

The perspective of the spiritual worker is to become what Sir John Templeton calls "unselfed," by which he means stepping away from ego. Being unselfed is a courageous, spiritually sustaining act that opens the door to communication in a way that considers other people.

In our fragmented, high-pressure, quick-fix world, holding on to self*less*ness is becoming harder to do. We are surrounded by greed. Success is measured by money, and money is used both as a means to purchase enjoyments and as a means to exert power and control. If the focus is all on self and the measure of value of self is solely material, then it is nearly impossible to sustain a spiritual center that sets aside ego. To the worker who craves a spiritual workplace, witnessing and being pulled into this relentless pursuit of material success is fragmenting and dispiriting (see the quote by Charles Brass, below).

Expressing Spirituality

"Since the Industrial Revolution, human beings have attached a special importance to the institutions of business and commerce to the continuing detriment of other human institutions. We have allowed ourselves to become seduced by the apparent capacity of business to create wealth and attached ourselves to workplaces with great abandon in an attempt to secure some of that wealth for ourselves.

"It is in the pursuit of that wealth that businesses and workplaces have moved increasingly away from any notions of spirituality. Until we are prepared to recognize the wealth created outside of the commercial world and develop ways in which this wealth can be captured and distributed, it is unlikely we will dismantle enough of our workplace infrastructure to allow expression of spirituality."

Source: Charles Brass, Chairman, Future of Work Foundation, Australia, in an interview with Ann Coombs, June 2000.

Fragmenting of self leads to a spiritual malaise. It is difficult to resist joining the pursuit of success when everyone around is engaged in it so busily and apparently so happily. The longing for spiritual nourishment is translated into a grasshopper-like pursuit for the quick fix and the latest spiritual trend. These things are momentarily satisfying, but like sugar highs they are fundamentally unsatisfying because they are fundamentally empty. The letdown comes quickly and with a *thump*.

The Search for Meaning

True spiritual nourishment comes from commitment to relationships based on accountability, responsibility and acceptance that perfection is a chimera. The quest for perfection—in self or in others—is by definition doomed. It is possible to mask the human realities of disappointment. It is possible to turn away from disaster when it strikes other people. But this will succeed only for a limited time, because eventually everyone is touched, one way or another, by the essence, the fullness, of life itself.

The only guarantee about life is that there is no guarantee. Yet everywhere we look, that is the expectation and the promise—guaranteed products, guaranteed services, guaranteed satisfaction. How can one resist joining the clamor for guaranteed happiness?

This, I think, is one of the factors driving people in pursuit of new religions. They are searching for a finer consciousness, possibly a better understanding of self and a measure of contentment. When the faith of choice cannot sustain the promise of joy or bring absolute release from worry, it is tempting to try another faith. When one's career, friends or family founder on the rocks of doubt or stress, it is tempting to change the arrangements rather than to think deeply and seriously about the underlying reality. It is tempting to keep chasing after the elusive magic bullet instead of dealing with the truth—that no one can know what is going to happen next and no one can insulate self from a life that includes pain as well as joy.

Some argue that the current quest for spiritual nourishment is really a by-product of immaturity. Maturity, they say, means growing up emotionally and accepting that uncertainty is an inescapable human condition. There are no guarantees. We can be born with more luck or less luck. We can be blessed with good fortune or be afflicted with tragedy at any moment. Maturity brings the emotional strength to deal with whatever comes. They argue that, given time to grow up, everyone will eventually find the maturity to understand and accept reality. The end point? There's no need to provide spiritual nourishment in the workplace. People will find it on their own in time.

This explanation certainly applies in some cases, but if one looks at the demographics of the current workforce, it does not hold. At the turn of this century, the population is heavily weighted toward people ages 45 and up. They have reached a stage of life that generally brings with it a measure of self-understanding, calmness and acceptance. But what they are experiencing is chaos, stress and weariness, and they are expressing these feelings in a longing for spiritual nourishment. Clearly, something fundamental is missing in North American society. The search for soulful meaning is continuing rather than abating.

I agree that maturity—or lack of maturity—is a factor of influence. I argue, however, that the issue of maturity is societal as well as individual. I believe the underlying issue is the growth of lack of accountability. As a society, we have become much more permissive, much more tolerant of conscienceless behaviors, and much more accepting of lack of accountability. I believe it is because we have lost our connection with our spiritual core. We have cut ourselves adrift from soul. We know there is something wrong because so much that surrounds us has become chaotic. We have become totally focused on self, but it has not brought us a true sense of peace.

So, we search for meaning, for a connection with our spiritual cores. Naturally, we look at every part of our lives. Our personal lives are our own responsibility, but what about spiritual meaning in our professional lives? Is it our employers' responsibility to provide it?

The Spiritual Workplace

What is a spiritual workplace, and who will create it? "A workplace that supports the worker's soul is not a place. It is a frame of thinking. And the workers themselves will create it," says Wendy

Greene, manager of Investor Communications at Hughes Electronics Corporation.

I am convinced that it is the employers' responsibility to trust, encourage and support the search for meaning with a new language and a new environment. It must come through a cultural transformation built on trust, because without trust one cannot have a spiritually supportive workplace or a spiritual workforce.

The emerging spiritual workers are honorable, authentic and steeped in integrity. They are coming to their workplaces with the desire to live according to these values and beliefs. They are looking for corporations that provide what they regard as a safe place, one in which they can be fully engaged.

Is it possible to provide a spiritually nourishing workplace, one in which individuals are valued as spiritual beings? Oh, yes, it is possible. In fact, this push from spiritually aware individuals bodes well for the new century. Corporations that continue to listen, develop and use a new language of inclusiveness and respect, and that are courageous enough to seize the opportunity that the search for spirituality presents, will do extremely well. By giving these workers a place where they can make a difference and *see* they are making a difference, these corporations will attract and keep the best talent and most committed individuals.

Will the size of the corporation make a difference? It may seem unreasonable to expect a business with 55,000 employees to value and honor each individual as a spiritual being. True, immense numbers make it harder, but the basic question is whether the organization has the courage and the honesty to create an environment conducive to overall spiritual well-being. Any attempt, however well meant, is unlikely to succeed with every individual, regardless of the size of the organization. But it will succeed with most *if* the attempt is genuine and sustained and *if* the language and actions are imbued with truth and respect.

It is difficult to overestimate the magnitude of the effort it will take to accomplish the objective of creating and maintaining a spiritually supportive workplace. The search for spiritual meaning is real, but it is occurring in a contradictory social climate that puts a high premium on avoiding suffering, pain, chaos and change, yet celebrates taking risks. Employers can be forgiven for being confused. What is the point of providing a spiritually supportive workplace if the people who say they want it are not truly willing to pay the price that it demands?

The answer is that one reaps what one sows. Corporations that really want to build a future of long-lasting value will provide spiritually nourishing workplaces, even if it seems the majority of workers appear unlikely to appreciate the effort, or understand it, or care. Some corporations know that if they provide a spiritually aware workplace, they will gradually attract individuals who sense they are missing something and who understand to some small degree the nature of what they are missing. It may be only because these individuals have tried the quick fixes and discovered those fixes have not worked, or because they suspect a quick fix does not bring lasting value or satisfaction. Whether or not they understand it, they are going to be drawn to workplaces that have more depth, just as they are going to be attracted to religions that provide more than just a good feeling from group chanting at sunrise once a week.

Invest in developing environments of regard, integrity, honesty and long-lasting value. Live with courage and speak a language of regard. It will take time, but once spiritually hungry workers have found these environments, they will be drawn to and nourished by the intrinsic qualities of spirituality, as seen in the list below. A truly living workplace is an inspiring, satisfying place of soul-sourced values.

The Truly Living Workplace

These characteristics are integrated into the truly living, spiritually supportive workplace:

- Respect
- Dignity
- Honor
- Honesty
- Acceptance
- Appreciation
- Truth
- Love
- Integrity

Spirit, Wisdom, Openness and Thoughtfulness

Training consultants and others who evaluate companies to determine the nature of their problems conduct their examinations by looking at what are conventionally referred to as SWOTs. In management consulting terms, SWOT stands for Strengths, Weaknesses, Opportunities and Threats.

In this century, change is needed. I suggest using different SWOTs to understand the dynamics and characteristics of spiritually living workplaces. In my company, the letters in SWOT stand for Spirit, Wisdom, Openness and Thoughtfulness. The SWOTs I conduct take participants to a very different level and provide a thought-provoking experience that is often an altering one.

My SWOT analysis is not a checklist. It is a framework, as shown on pages 135 to 140 for helping people articulate their hunger for spiritual meaning and understand how their workplaces support, or fail to support, their needs. Are these qualities—spirit, wisdom, openness and thoughtfulness—knit into the fabric of the workplace?

The SWOT Framework:
Spirit, Wisdom, Openness, Thoughtfulness
Leadership Qualities for a Living Workplace

A truly living workplace is a satisfying place that supports and nourishes Spirit, Wisdom, Openness and Thoughtfulness. This SWOT framework is designed to help you examine and articulate the degree to which your workplace is a truly living workplace.

The framework is divided into four parts: spirit, wisdom, openness and thoughtfulness. Twelve characteristics are listed for each. These characteristics describe qualities practiced by effective leaders who are committed to spirituality in the workplace. You are given four rating choices for each characteristic: Consistently, Often, Sometimes or Rarely.

When you use this framework, make every effort to be thoughtful, respectful and honest about your understanding of the person you are rating. Help yourself understand what you are seeking and finding in your workplace. Identify specific behaviors, statements or incidents that you have observed.

The first stage is to rate the individual according to the 12 characteristics in each category.

The second stage is to write a statement that answers this question: "Why did I rate this person's spirit (or openness or wisdom or thoughtfulness) in this way?"

The third stage is to write a concluding statement that summarizes your overall understanding of how this individual is affecting your workplace.

Your thoughtfulness and understanding will help you bring a degree of spiritual awareness forward for discussion, for understanding and for change.

Spiritual Framework

Spirit

	CONSISTENTLY	OFTEN	SOMETIMES	RARELY
Has a passion for goodness				
Is committed to speaking and acting upon the truth				
Encourages and refreshes others in their spirit—that is, lifts their spirit				
Believes in the people he or she manages or supervises				
Believes in the purpose of the organization or business				
Believes in the intrinsic value and honor of work				
Sees beyond obvious, material, mechanical working reality into the human values important to individuals on your team				
Is able to bring a sense of awe and spiritual understanding into your workplace				
Is able to draw others into a place of spiritual insight and belief that transcends the material world				
Is able to reinforce the integration of the immediate and the transcendent				
Supports people in and through their work				
Brings the vitality of spirit and soul into the workplace				

Why did you choose these ratings? Give a thoughtful, reasoned example for at least two characteristics on the Spirit list.

_____

_____

_____

_____

_____

© 2001. Ann Coombs and Elaine Pountney

Spiritual Framework

Wisdom

	CONSISTENTLY	OFTEN	SOMETIMES	RARELY
Has discernment—that is, shows insight and understanding into what seems obscure or hidden				
Sees what is really going on				
Sees beyond what is; keeps an eye on the horizon				
Understands consequences—that is, what will happen *if* . . .				
Calculates risks and gauges costs accurately in terms of both material and human resources				
Acts with clarity and purpose				
Knows what is right, not just what works				
Understands virtues and aims for moral excellence				
Builds on core human values				
Understands how and why people thrive and grow in the workplace				
Appreciates the complexity of life but is able to simplify and clarify				
Demonstrates respect for the sanctity of life, virtue and worth				

Why did you choose these ratings? Give a thoughtful, reasoned example for at least two characteristics on the Wisdom list.

_____

_____

_____

_____

_____

© 2001. Ann Coombs and Elaine Pountney

Spiritual Framework

Openness

	CONSISTENTLY	OFTEN	SOMETIMES	RARELY
Communicates clearly and concisely				
Communicates essential information to all persons who will be affected				
Gives honest, respectful answers				
Asks direct, genuine questions				
Makes face-to-face communication his or her first choice				
Is willing to listen with understanding when another person is talking				
Intentionally tries to find and understand the other person's point of view				
Gives feedback that enhances and supports professional and personal development of the other person				
Is willing to admit his or her own mistakes and limitations				
Is willing to be challenged as a leader				
Is committed to personal growth as a leader				
Is willing to acknowledge, celebrate and reward the success of others				

Why did you choose these ratings? Give a thoughtful, reasoned example for at least two characteristics on the Openness list.

_____

_____

_____

_____

© 2001. Ann Coombs and Elaine Pountney

Spiritual Framework

Thoughtfulness

	CONSISTENTLY	OFTEN	SOMETIMES	RARELY
Is kind				
Cares for people in your organization or company				
Actively builds a caring and humane environment in your workplace				
Is compassionate without ignoring accountability issues				
Understands that all business decisions have an impact on peoples' lives				
Looks for opportunities to express caring and compassion while upholding personal competency and economic competitiveness				
Has the capacity to look at the longer-term viability of the larger picture, including human, economic and environmental resources				
Cares about how the little pieces fit into the big picture				
Wonders about the immediate consequences of decisions now being made				
Thinks things through as an act of responsible thoughtfulness				
Takes time and makes space to think and to reflect				
Intentionally integrates both personal and company values into his or her specific leadership responsibilities				

Why did you choose these ratings? Give a thoughtful, reasoned example for at least two characteristics on the Thoughtfulness list.

_____

_____

_____

© 2001. Ann Coombs and Elaine Pountney

*

Spiritual Framework

In your view, is this person committed to and contributing to a truly living workplace? Write an honest, open statement that describes and summarizes how you understand and experience the overall impact this person is having on your workplace.

_____

_____
_____
_____
_____
_____
_____
_____
_____
_____
_____
_____
_____
_____
_____
_____
_____
_____
_____
_____
_____
_____
_____

© 2001. Ann Coombs and Elaine Pountney

Many managers do not realize that these qualities can be sensed immediately or in a very short time. Is the atmosphere imbued with them? Environments that lack them quickly show signs of the strains—plummeting morale and rising cynicism.

The best example I have from my own experience involved a large, international company. I was called in by the president who was concerned about the overall ethics and morale in the company. He was concerned, and he wanted to know how to fix the problems he perceived.

I began by talking to employees using my SWOT framework: Spirit, Wisdom, Openness and Thoughtfulness. I asked employees how they viewed the organization. I asked them what they felt was missing, if there was a course the company could or should be taking, what they would be doing if they were leading the company, what the most important things in their lives were, what mattered to them the most. I listened to what they were telling me, and I listened for what they were *not* telling me.

I quickly discovered that the president, who was married and had children, was engaged in an intimate relationship with one of his assistants and that the whole staff was aware of it. They resented being told to be honest and trustworthy when they saw him betraying his own family.

Within two days of starting my assignment, I returned to the president with a preliminary report. "We have a problem," I said. "Your issue is that you want total commitment based on loyalty, values and ethics, but you are apparently well known for having an affair with an assistant." He said, "I did not ask you to come in and tell me how to live my life. I asked you to come in and fix the problems in my company."

This president was unable to see the connection between his personal conduct and the ethical standard and commitment he demanded from his employees. His actions corroded his employees' respect and loyalty.

Spirit, Wisdom, Openness and Thoughtfulness are elements both employees and employers can consider to help themselves understand what they are seeking and what they are finding. But both need to bring to the table a degree of spiritual awareness and a willingness to be honest with themselves.

The Courageous CEO

It takes a courageous, intuitive leader of conscience and consciousness to develop an atmosphere of Spirit, Wisdom, Openness and Thoughtfulness. Chances are that a leader who is prepared to accept the results of my form of SWOT analysis has already developed a spiritually supportive workplace or understands how to encourage employees to contribute to a caring atmosphere.

Starting from a clean slate is always easier, but realistically speaking few CEOs have that luxury. Leaders are more likely to come into corporations that have established characters, views and, possibly, religious affiliations. Reshaping the environment is challenging under any circumstances, but it is particularly challenging if the CEO has been brought in to effect radical change, the character of the corporation is dysfunctional, or there is discomfort in the workforce because the company has been growing so quickly that employees are virtually strangers to each other. The challenge will be accentuated if early or recent decisions need to be reversed. It can be done successfully, but only if it is done with honesty.

Employees will respond to leadership of integrity and vision. They may not be able to point to what it is that makes integrity and vision. They may not be able to articulate it. They may be reacting only at a deep, subconscious level. But they will react positively and appreciatively to the atmosphere of a truly spiritually supportive workplace.

Values in Action

When Marilyn Knox of Nestlé Canada is asked about spirituality in the workplace, she says she sees it as values in action. She describes values in action as more than just an absence of fear. She talks about spirituality cradling values in a way that encourages workers to come forward freely with their own values.

Knox led a workplace exercise in which she addressed the values of her team. She began by giving her employees an opportunity to express their individual values, to discuss those that they regarded in their lives, and to give opinions about how they find them in their workplace.

The values Knox's employees listed included *maturity, respect, integrity, caring* and *purpose*. She collated the results and held two employee-centered discussions to discuss the values in the context of the Nutrition Division and others for the company as a whole. She helped employees focus on behaviors that demonstrated these values in action.

The result, in part, was that the employees changed their environment by examining behaviors that supported their shared values. One example was a change to a totally open-concept office with no walls and with Knox among them. Nondesignated workstations were also set aside so that employees who work offsite had a place to work on the days they were onsite. Interestingly, within a year of conducting and implementing the results of this values exercise, the Nutrition Division become the fastest growing department in the company.

Moments of Truth

Looking at self with balance, truth and honesty is more difficult than it appears to be. Nearly all of us share the natural human tendency to overstate or understate our qualities and skills; we overlook our flaws or give them too much weight. It is the rare person who has the gift to look at self with truly objective eyes, mind and heart.

For many of us, clarity comes as a result of a moment of truth. Truth comes in all guises at unexpected times from surprising quarters. The moment of truth might just as easily be the result of a chance, offhand remark or of a personally shattering event. It might be happy or unhappy, good or bad, comic or tragic. Whatever its guise, the moment of truth is one that creates change. It is not simply a matter of the scales dropping from one's eyes. It is a matter of insight and change as a result of that insight.

An epiphany, a powerful moment of truth, is a definitive spiritual insight that is more than just a realization of the need for change. It is a spiritual moment that brings with it the demand for change.

Of course, an individual may not act on the insight. Some will integrate the insights into their lives. Others will vow to do so and then leave them behind along with the memory of the event, especially if the event was unpleasant or unhappy. For example, a worker experiences an incident that brings home with sudden clarity that he or she must bring truthfulness, ethics and values to the workplace. The worker realizes that even though the company is being open and honest, he or she has not been personally upholding these values as fully as possible. What will that worker choose to do? Accept personal responsibility and accountability?

Every individual must accept the responsibility of being connected to something larger than the limits of his or her own life. Every individual must bring compassion, caring and truth to the workplace. Every individual must accept that there is no such thing as perfection, that there is often conflict and chaos, that change is inevitable and that corporate leaders are struggling, in addition, with issues that affect economic well-being.

Courage and Risk

Individuals have to ask themselves if they are willing to be courageous and, if so, to what extent. They must be able to accept the concept of risk. And they must be able to accept the idea of being sustained by something that goes beyond the conventional expectations and definitions of success.

The essence of the question is what an individual is prepared to do if the company is unable to provide a workplace that is entirely safe and spiritually nourishing. For individuals to answer this question in a valid way, they must have a solid, soulful connection to what is truly important for personal well-being. With a solid connection, individuals will have the courage and strength to take responsibility for acting on convictions about what constitutes a spiritually supportive workplace and for accepting the personal consequences of those actions.

Without a solid, soulful connection, individuals will find it difficult to sustain themselves in a workplace that does not provide all the spiritual support they wish for. They will have difficulty finding the strength or courage to initiate or accept change in either their own circumstances or the larger environment. For them, epiphanies will become moments of danger rather than opportunities for spiritual growth.

This conundrum is particularly challenging for human resources professionals, who are usually charged with implementing policies that may well have been developed by leaders disconnected or insulated from day-to-day turmoil. I have observed that most human resources departments in major corporations today are not given the encouragement or support they need to develop spiritually nourishing workplaces. Their mandate is more likely to be limited to creating harmony. This is certainly a positive characteristic, but it is usually defined in a very limited way.

Keeping the peace is one thing; providing the framework for genuine, truthful, soulful peace is another. The irony is that *peacelovers*, because they are anxious to maintain every appearance of peace, may abdicate their responsibility to encourage the development of a spiritually nourishing workplace. [By contrast, *peacemakers* are courageous risk-takers who provide insights that may result in short-term discomfort, but which ultimately support lasting harmony.]

Humility and Compromise

Intuitive ability and discernment are now being recognized as strengths. They bring valuable opportunities that can be harnessed to support conventional corporate objectives. But how can workers align their values with their jobs if the corporate commitment to spirituality is not as fundamental and secure as they need it to be?

Everywhere we look, we see signs of insincerity and superficiality, even within traditional churches. Marketing campaigns promoting heaven, soul and spirit abound. There is talk of the importance of tolerant, values-based lives. But for all that, societal standards have not changed much from the creed of greed. In fact, if anything, the world has become a harder, less forgiving place. The poor are penalized for being poor, welfare rates are reduced, children go to school hungry, and the unemployed or unemployable are dismissed as lazy or unworthy. And yes, the glass ceiling for women still exists.

It is an uneasy time for both corporations and workers. Both owe themselves and each other responsibility and accountability. For corporations, it needs to be expressed in genuine commitment and clear communications that address bedrock values and expectations. For employees, it needs to be expressed as a willingness to understand and collaborate. Both need to accept the degrees to which they can and should exercise control, from a spiritual perspective, over their own choices about how to live. Both must look at what is within their power to change, what they want to change and what risks they are prepared to take in pursuing their commitment to change.

The challenge is to find a balance between control and support that works for individuals as well as for the collective. It is impossible to achieve in environments governed by fear. It is possible in living workplaces with environments governed by spirit, wisdom, openness and thoughtfulness.

The starting point is acknowledging that there is a power greater than any individual, and accepting that we are connected to something or someone greater than ourselves. A sense of awe and an embracing of our humanity open the channel to truth and spirituality. The higher we are in the food chain, however, the more difficult this may be. CEOs who run $100-million businesses are treated with such deference and admiration at every turn, they are unlikely to be awed by very much. They may find it difficult to see themselves as no more and no less valuable than the smallest cog in the corporate wheel. And yet it is these high-powered leaders who must lead the way to deep, genuine commitment to providing spiritual sustenance for those who depend on them, as well as for themselves.

It takes enormous courage to look at self in the naked state of imperfection and vulnerability. Having created and lived by images of success, power and control, it is extremely frightening for such leaders to think about letting them go.

Balancing Realities

How can one balance the realities of corporate life and the truth of what it takes to move forward as a spiritually sustained individual? How can one set aside ego and remain optimistic and spiritually sustained in a corporate environment where symbols of status carry enormous significance? How can one find courage, trust and truth within?

Few can just open their minds, invite wisdom and thoughtfulness, and understand that living within one's spirit is paradoxically very simple. Some are fortunate to find sustenance in daily gratitude for the gifts of life and another day. Others find inner courage to live their convictions as a result of an epiphany that forces them to recognize that they cannot continue living as they do. All are affected by the language that surrounds them in the workplace. They will cringe if the language is challenging, negative, aggressive—or relentlessly positive. The fear and dishonesty threaded into the language will intimidate all but the most emotionally and spiritually secure.

Even in a spiritually sustaining workplace, it will be difficult to maintain equilibrium, because even the strongest traditions of respect, compassion and courtesy can be damaged or destroyed by ill will on the part of a few, if those few are in positions of authority. It will be much easier if everyone brings respect, honesty and courtesy, examines differences of opinion, finds accommodation and balance, and makes a sincere effort to integrate personal values in a way that contributes to the life of the corporation as well as to the individual.

Filling the Void

What people find and experience in the workplace environment greatly affects their personal quest for spiritual sustenance, if only because they spend so much of their time at work. But more than that, the work we do and the people with whom we work are still the way most of us define ourselves, because it is where we express ourselves and where we spend a great deal of our emotion, intellect and energy.

Workers who are committed to living ethically and truthfully will be disturbed by corporate environments where high-sounding principles are not being taken seriously. Some will interpret it as betrayal. They will leave, taking their talents, skills and commitment with them. Others will learn to live with the pain. They may not leave, but they will not be wholly engaged. They will lose enthusiasm, react with apathy rather than excitement, and settle for the mediocre in everything, including their own performance and fulfilling their own potential. When the tough times come, they will not be able to offer the strength or commitment the corporation needs to respond effectively.

Finding Truth

What is truth? Is it something written in stone and the same for all? Or is truth a variation depending on one's circumstances, the way one was brought up, one's religious view or lack of religious view?

For me, living in truth provides the soul with much needed nourishment and resilience. Truth is real and compelling wherever it is found. Without truth you can not have a workplace that is supportive.

Wherever we find our truth and whatever its nature, we must live it with a full heart. As British theologian C.H. Spurgeon said more than 100 years ago, "There must be vigor, power, freshness, reality, eagerness and warmth about it, or it will be good for nothing."

That is why, when truth is abandoned, the workplace deadens.

Truth is seizing the opportunity to accept epiphanies as valuable gifts. Truth is making a commitment to look at who one is and, beyond toward that which is greater than ourselves. Truth is linked to how one is living one's life. It is understanding that if the "who" and the "how" are allowed to diverge, the soul will be pulled apart.

"A passionate heart
overcomes fear
and pain with joy
and love."

Ann Coombs

CHAPTER 8

The Passionate Heart

Twenty-first century workers are seeking increased personal fulfillment in all facets of their lives. For many, this means including spiritual well-being in their professional lives.

Some are looking to what philosopher Mark Kingwell calls "techno-spirituality." In *Dreams of Millennium: Report From a Culture on the Brink,* Kingwell reports this based on his own experience: "Rejecting Christian faith can create a troubling vacuum at one's spiritual centre, as I soon discovered, and into this vacuum can rush all kinds of ideas, both soothing and terrifying. When traditional answers no longer aid us, the new, sometimes twisted forms of religiosity characteristic of our day find fertile ground. So, too, does a misplaced faith in the power of human reason we call scientism—reaching at a peak the sort of arrogant techno-spirituality espoused by the gurus of *Wired* magazine. Neither of these is an adequate response to the challenges of the approaching millennium."[33]

Some are taking refuge in what Paulina Borsook, author of

Cyberselfish: A Critical Romp Through the Terribly Libertarian Culture of High Tech, calls "techno-libertarianism." She defines this as an ego-driven philosophy based on the conviction that the technologically and economically superior are also personally superior.

Some are hoping their employers will provide a spiritually supportive environment. Others are choosing to seek it on their own. They are walking into self-employment in the belief that they will be able to create more satisfaction in their lives. Both employees and the self-employed want to exercise a greater degree of control over the part of their future that can be within their grasp. They realize that they must accept pain, as well as joy, with spirit and courage. They hope their reward will be living in a fully engaged way.

How are corporate leaders, workers and entrepreneurs in the living workplace of the 21st century finding their way? What is the source of their courage? What are the qualities they need to bring their dreams to life? What does living in a fully engaged way mean? What is the role of the passionate heart?

Being and Dreaming

We learn much by living and working with others and by seeing our experiences reflected in the mirror of other people's comments and reactions. But when we are placed in an environment without external noise, distraction or stimulation, we have a magnificent opportunity to discover much about who we truly are and to gain precious wisdom.

It was in a silent retreat with the blessings of uninterrupted meditation and prayer, for example, that I discovered the power and dimensions of truth. The retreat gave me an understanding of how powerful life can be when self-importance is set aside. I also came to a fuller understanding that knowledge is not truth. Facts are important, but they are of limited value unless they are touched and shaped by a connection to the human spirit. As well, I grasped something I have often had occasion to remember. As I later noted in my journal, *Following the truth in spite of all the challenges will take us where we need to be, even though it may not be a place of choice.* Focusing on finding the truth is important, but sometimes the resulting changes are not particularly desirable. The changes, however, take us where we need to be, although we may not fully appreciate it at the time.

The need to seek the truth never ends because truth is something that reveals itself incrementally. There may be great, blinding flashes of insight, but truth might be revealed just as easily by a casual remark from an acquaintance. It may be something so small as to seem insignificant at the time. If one is not totally driven to know the truth, one may well miss both the insight and the significance of the insight. To appreciate, understand and accept the insight, one must be open, present and vulnerable. One must be ready.

For those who seek the insights and wisdom of self-discovery, it is essential to provide the time and space for contemplation. Entrepreneurs in particular need a period of calmness to listen to their souls, hearts and minds. They need time to dream, without interruption, noise or distractions, without demands to do or be, before tackling the actualization of something that may seem ephemeral.

Because contemplative time is a luxury in our hurried world, taking time to dream requires a belief that it will be valued. For those with professional, financial or moral obligations, it can be extremely difficult to explain and justify. Even for those who are able to set aside obligations to others for a time, the internally generated pressure to perform and produce may be too great.

For workers being urged by their employers to act more like entrepreneurs while remaining part of the corporation, it is perhaps even more difficult. Corporate managers do not always understand that creativity and innovation cannot be called up on demand. Thinking and dreaming are unlikely to yield the desired results when external time limits are imposed, creative thinking is not truly encouraged, and high expectations are pre-set.

Yet that thinking and dreaming time is essential because dreams lure individuals to leave the known and explore the unknown. The process involves stepping away from the comfort zone and daring to examine hopes hidden in the heart, mind and soul.

Mind-set

There are many books and other resources that offer suggestions for making the transition to an entrepreneurial way of thinking and acting. My focus, however, has always been the soul, mind and heart of the person moving in the direction of self-discovery and being drawn toward fundamental change. The inherent promises are often enticingly contradictory.

One promise is that being entrepreneurial brings unmatched blessings and gifts in a world made more attractive because it is largely of one's own making. This is true. It is a great gift to be able to work with personal integrity, passion, care, inspiration, innovation and joy. It is a great blessing to be able to exercise judgment, bring a unique vision and make choices about the day-to-day matters that make up the texture and passion of one's life.

Another promise is that being entrepreneurial brings stress, worry and uncertainty. This is also true. Decisions must be made and consequences accepted, whether good or bad. Responsibility and accountability cannot be shifted elsewhere or ignored.

Some entrepreneurs strike out on their own and create successful new businesses, services or products. They take justifiable pride in measuring their success in financial terms. For others, the rewards are measured in smaller, less material ways. The gifts and blessings are the option to decide what, when, with whom and how hard to work, the option to pause and smell the roses, to enjoy the sunshine on a beautiful day, to read bedtime stories to their children, to be excited when they start work every day, and to have the immense satisfaction of well-earned achievements.

For the entrepreneurial individuals who continue to work in a corporate context, the reward may be creating initiatives or developing processes that bring substantive success to themselves and to their employers.

Whatever the measure or the context, the great lure of the entrepreneurial model is the ability to live in integrity and provide solace for the heart, mind, spirit and soul.

Sharing in Growth

Entrepreneur-leaders derive satisfaction from gaining a significant measure of control over their lives. But as they build their businesses and expand their workforces, are they able to provide the same reward for their employees?

Some are able and willing to try, and some succeed brilliantly. Others are unable to do so for a number of reasons. As businesses grow in size and importance, for example, financial, management and administrative obligations also grow. Entrepreneur-leaders must rely more and more on others to keep the wheels turning. Another natural consequence is that organizational structures evolve into more complex forms. By definition, workers are gradually required to conform to rules and meet expectations set for them by supervisors. But because entrepreneur-leaders are likely to maintain personal freedom of action, they may not realize that their employees are not enjoying the same benefit.

It has been said that the only way to ensure an equitable sharing of the gifts and blessings of the entrepreneurial model is to keep companies small. When the numbers on the payroll grow, so do the difficulties in providing the atmosphere that nourishes souls. Discovering and protecting a life of joys and blessings is challenged by the corporate juggernaut.

This is likely to change in the living workplace of the 21st century, however. As spiritually aware workers grow in number and influence, all employers—large and small—will be challenged to find ways to give their employees greater authority and freedom of movement. Ten or more years down the line, staying small may not necessarily be the optimal way to remain caring and compassionate. In fact, entrepreneur-leaders who meet the challenge effectively are likely to find it easier to maintain and share the precious spirit across their companies while continuing to grow.

The Power of the Heart

We all hope to experience passion in our lives, but not everyone in the workplace is able to express it or is encouraged to do so (see the quote by Charles Brass, below). But how many realize they have the capacity for passion? How do they define it? How would they choose to express it if given the encouragement? How many are courageous enough to express it even when encouraged? What constitutes encouragement in the corporate environment?

Expressing Passion

"Human passion is a fascinating phenomenon. Human beings appear profoundly programmed to explore and express passion throughout their lives. While it is true that the world of jobs and employment has done its very best to dampen this passion (for at least eight hours per day), people nonetheless seem to find ways to maintain it somewhere else in their lives.

"It is also true that there is an increasing trend toward the ingestion of various chemical substances (such as alcohol, tobacco and chocolate) as a substitute for a more direct expression of passion, and perhaps this has something to do with the difficulty of switching from the deliberately non-passionate world of the job to a passionate expression of life at the end of each business day.

"There is nothing about a technological workplace which inspires passion. However, there is also no reason (except a failure of human imagination) why a technological workplace could not be shaped to provide an outlet for passion."

Source: Charles Brass, Chairman, Future of Work Foundation, Australia, in an interview with Ann Coombs, June 2000.

Some managers appear to believe that just telling people to be passionate about their work should be enough, when, in fact, it is unrealistic and unproductive. How long can employees sustain their energy, for example, when writing code alone in a cubicle for weeks at a time or working in an atmosphere that discourages unfettered thinking and dreaming?

The passionate heart will thrive in corporations driven by change at any and all levels. An environment of change is part of what enables a passionate heart to emerge, because change, and taking enjoyment in the change, ignites and intensifies the passion.

Passion is about freedom and faith. Only with freedom of spirit and faith in a power beyond oneself is it possible to know the most profound and deepest inner peace. A passionate heart brings with it the strength, daring and courage to defend the spirit and live the faith.

The mark of the true entrepreneur—whether a corporate leader, self-employed consultant, volunteer in the not-for-profit sector, or a stay-at-home parent—is entirely committed to a personal vision rooted deeply in a powerful, empowering heart. The vision is always one of living fully, with depth, nurturing and the ability to question self without ever doubting personal integrity or authenticity. The passionate heart derives its power from the determination to be honest, authentic and guided by caring.

The corporate leaders who will be most successful in the living workplace of the 21st century will have passionate hearts, freedom of spirit, faith and inner peace. They will be the creators, innovators and communicators. Their joyfulness, enthusiasm and energy will attract the most prized workers. They will succeed in bringing the corporate vision to glittering life and sustaining it in the face of global competition and continuing technological and societal change.

Leaders who lack an awareness of passion within their beings will likely be less successful. High degrees of business skills and overall strategies will not be sufficient to offset the lack of passion. If they are without the gift of passion themselves, they will be far less able to inspire and motivate. They will find it difficult to communicate their enthusiasm much beyond those with whom they are in direct contact.

Encouraging Passion

If corporations truly want their employees to be entrepreneurial—to be passionate, creative, innovative and excited about their work—they must meet the challenge of encouraging employees to express their passion. Entrepreneur-leaders must recognize the need to look at their workers as individuals with hearts, talents and ideas, and must find ways to encourage workers to bring their personal passions to bear on their work. Gifted leaders will find those ways, and workers with passionate hearts will gravitate to places where they sense an opportunity to bring their excitement and inspiration to their work.

Philip E. Donne, president of Cossette Communications, believes in the value of purposeful play. Purposeful play is arranging creative, play-based activities while ensuring that the play comes to a conclusion relevant to a workplace goal. He also believes in the benefits of social interaction, which he defines as encouraging employees to mix in social as well as professional settings. In all interactions, he says, it's important to engage employees in activities that involve physical, emotional, spiritual and intellectual elements.

One purposeful play technique I have used is the List of Joys Workshop. The basic idea is simple. Individuals are asked to write a list of things that make them feel joyful or bring them satisfaction. When they're finished, I encourage them to share their lists. Over the years, I have observed that the lists feature everything from ice cream to romantic love, bungee jumping, tropical sunsets and walking on a sandy beach. What very rarely makes any list is some activity or experience related to work. The challenge for corporate leaders in the living workplace is to find creative ways to make life at work as joyful as life away from work.

Another purposeful play technique I have used is the Living Fearlessly Workshop. Again, the basic idea is simple. Individuals participate in an off-site, innovative and designed activity. It might be anything from a wilderness expedition to a day at an amusement park. One goal is to give participants an opportunity to discover within themselves a capacity or capability they did not realize or appreciate. Another objective is to help them develop a degree of sensitivity toward colleagues.

Whatever the activity, the Living Fearlessly Workshop requires careful preparation, including an opportunity for participants to table their doubts and fears. It also requires close monitoring and support during the activity, especially for those who are not able to finish. The workshop leader must be skilled in alleviating the impact of what may be interpreted as an embarrassing or humiliating failure.

In the many Living Fearlessly Workshops I have conducted, the results have always been interesting and significant. With one group of senior managers, for example, I began with a tour of Alcatraz. After walking them through a workshop entitled Prisons of the Mind and debriefing in the recreational area, we moved to a nearby beach. There, the managers were charged with creating a new model for their company. They weren't given any of the usual aids, such as flip charts and white boards. They could use only materials they found on the beach.

These managers came up with many exciting innovations. For

example, they used sand to represent the human resources department because they wanted to develop a department that was evolving and changing. They used a very large, heavy rock to represent the CEO to emphasize that their leader must be stable and secure at all times. They were excited by their model and eager to start implementing it. The feedback I got later was that that, in fact, happened.

Purposeful play techniques like these yield positive results only if the corporate leaders endorse and support them with complete enthusiasm. When they hold back, the effort is wasted. I recall one Living Fearlessly Workshop experience in which the president arrived late and refused to participate although he had commissioned the workshop. At the first break, we went outside to discuss his overall impressions of the workshop and what the result might be if he didn't participate himself. He hadn't realized that by remaining a spectator he might be giving a negative signal. He had merely been trying to avoid interrupting the activity already in progress. After the break, he got totally involved. Thanks to his concern for his employees, the workshop provided long-term value after all, despite the slightly shaky start.

Carefully crafted workshops like these are excellent ways to free the passion within individuals *if* the activities are presented in a regarding way and *if* everyone goes into them with open minds and hearts. They are also useful for helping workers define and deal with the fears and hesitations that are preventing them from being full contributors, especially if there has been good advance communication by management about what participants can expect. Eventually, through debriefing and guided discussion, participants are often able to discover new knowledge that they can bring to their work and their lives.

Competitive Collaboration

Few people describe entrepreneurs as collaborative. They visualize entrepreneurs as having total control over their lives and often working alone. I believe, however, that true entrepreneurs must understand collaboration if they are to succeed as the 21st-century marketplace evolves.

Corporations have used teamwork and project management for a long time. In the 20th century, however, project management or a team approach usually implied someone in charge to direct and shape the outcome.

As attitudes toward work change, definitions and interpretations of teamwork and project management are changing as well. The nature of collaboration is evolving. As a result, it is becoming just as important for entrepreneurial success as energy, initiative, independence and creativity have always been. The value of the collaboration is now being seen not just as the result of a team's work but also in the creation of the collaboration itself. It is an entity with value of its own.

Steven Zeisler, founder and director of Zeisler Associates, Inc., describes the evolving collaborative model in fluid terms. "You still need a leader, but the leader is a series of flexible roles that change quickly as the conditions do. You still need muscle, but it will be applied precisely, more judiciously, and it will be leveraged with widely distributed knowledge. You still need people, but they will be multifaceted, capable of autonomy and interdependence, thinking and doing, making their way to the place where they can help the most, applying judgment and creativity."

For entrepreneurs working on their own, the collaborative approach is likely to mean joining pods of like-minded professionals who rely on each other with trust and regard, contribute expertise, share knowledge, complete projects, and then move on into new and probably very different creative pods. There will still be a team leader or project manager, someone who is primarily responsible for liaison with the client, but all team members will be seen as equal, and results will be judged on the basis of client satisfaction, their own satisfaction and the satisfaction of all members of the pod.

Futurist Stephen Millett of Battelle's Energy Products Division suggests that the comparable corporate model may be what he calls "guerilla units." Corporations will form small, self-contained units with commanders and a hierarchy of authority. The units will move as needed to work on specific projects, much the way the Japanese *shusha* teams worked so successfully in developing and commercializing new products. Another possibility, he says, is "matrix management," where a few managers in charge of infrastructure (space, budgets, people and other resources) will work with team leaders who are charged with carrying through client-specific and project-specific missions.

Canadian tech-business futurist Tod Maffin predicts a shift that will also put employees and entrepreneurs together in neighborhood work centers. "Inside these centers, people who work for a variety of different companies or on their own will work in a shared environment. These work centers will also provide a quick way to start an on-line company with nearly no computer experience: rent a space, sit down and take an on-line questionnaire, then pick from a list of ready-to-go, on-line businesses." We see this as the future corporate "hotel."

The evolution toward the entrepreneurial model is likely to be more difficult for workers accustomed to and comfortable with the support of the corporate culture. Employees who are moving toward an entrepreneurial-style future, within the corporation or on their own, will have to accept that collaboration in some form will likely be necessary and advantageous. They will have to develop collaborative skills, even if they do not yet fully understand what this means or why it is important.

At the same time, to be successful in the 21st century, the entrepreneurial model must accept and integrate the competitiveness factor. There are always plenty of suppliers available to provide products and services. In the rough-and-tumble of the marketplace, collaboration and competition are constantly in play. Competition is in charge when going after a contract or a new customer. Collaboration is in charge when fulfilling the contract or serving a customer over the long term. But the lines are often blurred.

Today's competitor may also be today's collaborator, needed and welcomed in both roles.

Present Sense

Minimizing risk is good advice for the small-scale entrepreneur and the large-scale corporation alike. There is nothing to be gained and everything to lose from taking foolish risks.

For the true entrepreneur-leader, however, risk is just another factor in the decision mix. It is never enough on its own to stop the forward drive. Risk is always outweighed by the need to live fully and to give one's heart and passion scope to grow.

True entrepreneur-leaders must live sharply and clearly in the present sense. They cannot be dedicated and absent; the two states of mind are mutually exclusive. Living fully in the heart is the key to achieving joy and internal knowing. Entrepreneur-leaders are driven by self, ego, determination and pride to seek the internal knowing of being fully present, fully alive, fully committed, fully dedicated, fully aware, fully passionate and fully blessed. They measure success by this internal knowing. To them it is, ultimately, the only yardstick that matters and the only risk worth taking.

Conscious Character

My belief is that you cannot have a passionate heart if you have a speck of self-deception in your character. A truly passionate heart is a truthful and honest one.

More than 50 years ago, scientist and philosopher Emmet Fox talked about honesty as the first step to self-development. "Know what you really like," he advised in *Find and Use Your Inner Power*. "Know what you really want. Be honest with yourself. It may be that your taste in certain directions needs to be improved, but, if so, set out to improve it honestly and without self-deception."[34]

Entrepreneur-leaders are drivers, doers, leaders, innovators and risk-takers. They make conscious decisions based on values they perceive as absolutely critical to their survival as human beings with souls and spirits, hearts and minds.

Integrity and Ethics

Not long ago, the major media sneered at the term "consultant" as a euphemism for "unemployed." In fact, this view still prevails behind closed doors in some corporate boardrooms.

It is a problem for entrepreneurs for a number of reasons. One is simply the feeling of fragility mixed with the worry and excitement of standing alone amidst corporate giants. Anything that attacks the personal psyche is serious. The other is the reality for many entrepreneurs, especially those just starting out. Their best prospects for initial business are their former employers or networks of corporate contacts.

It is also a problem for employees being pushed to adopt the entrepreneurial model. An attitude of contempt seeping from the corporate boardroom inevitably contaminates the working atmosphere and casts doubt on the truthfulness underlying the company's directives.

True entrepreneurs get through this attitude by calling on their passion, faith, self-respect, resilience, self-reliance, pride and determination. There was a time when women who started businesses in their homes made gift baskets. They were not taken seriously as consultants who brought expertise or knowledge to corporations. Today, SOHO (small office/single owner, home office) entrepreneurs are developing a cachet of sorts. In this century, entrepreneurs can take comfort from a growing attitude of acceptance and respect. But until the attitude changes completely, entrepreneurs have to rely on their passion to keep true to their vision and create work that is meaningful to others.

What will hurry this along is the need for knowledge workers. This will be good news for entrepreneurs who have the knowledge, skills and integrity to respond to corporate needs. Those who will succeed in the longer term will be entrepreneurs who consistently demonstrate their integrity, authenticity, dedication, expertise and ethics. Consultants who abuse the trust placed in them—and there will always be some who do—will be revealed for what they are because competition will be stiffer. This will be the good news for corporations relying on external assistance or encouraging their employees to adopt an entrepreneurial approach.

Trust and Truth

It is difficult to maintain a passionate heart in the workplace. The average senior manager, for example, reads one million words a week. Information overload is exhausting. Finding the energy to remain passionate or the strength to live in a fully engaged way is a challenge in these circumstances.

The same is true for many entrepreneurs working outside corporations. Although they have a better chance to exert control over their lives, many fall into the trap of being so excited and engaged by their work that they ignore other balancing and nourishing parts of life.

Living in a fully engaged way means accepting joy as well as pain. It means accepting and setting aside worry. If one is living in a fully engaged way, one looks very closely at all the challenges and is totally honest about one's feelings. The disengaged way is to ignore the worry, pretend the worries do not exist, or mask worry in order to still the restless soul.

For many—employee or entrepreneur—the driving force of life is longing to unleash their passion. They understand it is passion that gives human beings optimism, joy and love. They want to be recognized for the passionate beings they are or can be. They want to talk about the deeper, thought-provoking questions of life. They want to talk about love. They want to connect with the passion in their hearts, and they want to connect their passion with all around them.

They want to trace a line between trust and truth, and they want to do it in whatever workplace context they find themselves.

The Joyful Life

The passionate heart evolves through experience, wisdom and a desire to be open to experiences and feelings.

I have been blessed with the privilege of working with many corporate leaders who have unleashed their passionate hearts and souls. Several years ago, for example, I was keynote speaker at a conference in New Orleans. One evening, my host took me and other guests to dinner at a sumptuously decorated restaurant that featured many mirrored walls. While trying to find a washroom, one of our party, a high-energy manager, walked straight into a mirror. "Oh, don't I know you?" was his immediate reaction. I still remember that incident as delightfully revealing, because I believe the journey through life includes laughter and laughter is part of a passionate soul.

Shortly after returning from the conference, I received a large pizza box at my office. Inside the lid, this manager had written an invitation to do a project with his company. My staff and I dropped everything to put together a proposal, write it on a mirror, put the mirror inside the box, and ship the box back that same day. We have worked together many times since, and we have become good and close friends.

Many people would just say, "Oh, funny guy," and get on with the serious business of work and life. But I see this manager's approach as demonstrating something fundamental about his character. When he walked into the mirror and when he sent me the pizza box, he signaled his deep sense of joyfulness and his courage in giving his passionate heart free rein.

The Fully Engaged Life

For me, living in a fully engaged way means living in a way that serves others. I define serving others as having responsibility for others and accepting that responsibility. In other words, it is essential to serve others in the context of an ethical and moral vision.

For me, living in a fully engaged way also means looking for, understanding and accepting fundamental truths and measuring myself by them. It means asking myself hard questions: What price am I prepared to pay for my soul? What price am I prepared to pay if I believe there is an eternal life? My answers depend a good deal on the tenets of my religious faith.

If I did not have a religious faith and I did not believe that there is eternal life, then I would also believe there are no consequences or accountability beyond my last breath on this Earth.

For me, truth is eternal, fundamental and unchanging. If I allow myself to change the rules whenever something I do not like comes up, at what point do I become accountable to something greater than myself? Will I ever, indeed, make that connection?

I believe that to live a fully engaged life, I must give without expectation of return, I must accept truth as eternal and unchanging, and I must never feel free to redefine truth to suit the circumstances of the moment. I also believe all of us must find and hold on to a shared vision of truth, heart, soul and spirit.

The Passionate Heart

The passionate heart is a noble one. It is magnanimous in the sense of having a greatness of mind and a generosity of spirit. By creating a sense of strength in self, it creates a sense of strength in others. Thus, the passionate heart has the power to heal wounded souls.

This kind of heart is honorable, principled and vulnerable. If we work with passionate hearts, our vulnerability will be recognized by ourselves and by others as true strength. It takes enormous courage to be vulnerable because it opens us to the judgments and criticisms of others. Living with a passionate heart brings the inner strength to sustain that vulnerability, to discover and explore, and to be adventuresome.

By being aware, the passionate heart creates and supports an ennobling, honoring environment, one that allows others to have an opportunity to discover the passion in their own hearts.

Corporate leaders who are of noble mind and heart allow the people around them to be magnanimous. They understand that this magnanimity will create the truest form of freedom and faith within the workplace. The company will flourish because everyone will realize their full potential and live more satisfying and interesting lives. A passionate heart is a loving heart. Living with a passionate heart is about living with love, expressing love, feeling love and spreading love. It is about having the capacity to love and giving oneself the freedom to love. It is about living a deliberate life. It is about acting on the passion and truth within. It is about allowing others to see passion and truth, and encouraging them to express their passions and truths. It is about bringing brightness and joy to life, strength and courage to the spirit, and comfort to the soul.

The passionate heart speaks with a new language that integrates words and actions and connects them to the soul. One hears words and senses meanings that include blessings, gifts, eternal values, deeds, bravery, grace, service, freshness, clarity, eagerness, compassion and significance.

The passionate heart acts with deepest humility. It makes commitments in the right spirit and for the right reasons. Living with this kind of heart is the greatest of all wealths because it allows people to find strength, courage and inner peace.

I have faith in the integrity of the human soul, the resilience of the human spirit, and the passion of the human heart. I believe that individuals in the living workplace of the 21st century will make a conscious choice to live in a fully engaged way with integrity, truth, compassion and trust. I believe the world will be made better by them.

Endnotes

1 From "The Future of Work: Career Evolution," *The Economist*, January 29, 2000.

2 From "Job Sculpting: The Art of Retaining Your Best People," *Harvard Business Review*, September–October, 1999.

3 See "America's Forgotten Majority," by Joel Rogers and Ruy Teixeira, *Atlantic Monthly*, June 2000, p. 68.

4 See "Want a job with those fries?" by Simon Houpt, *Globe and Mail*, June 17, 2000, p. R3.

5 From the U.S. Department of Labor, *Futurework: Trends and Challenges for Work in the 21st Century*, Executive Summary, September 1999.

6 June 12, 2000.

7 From *Exclusion & Embrace: A Theological Exploration of Identity, Otherness, and Reconciliation*, by Miroslav Volf. Nashville: Abingdon Press, 1996, p. 235.

8 From an interview with David Rousseau, November 1998.

9 In "Emerging HR Issues for the Twenty-first Century, *Employment Relations Today*, Winter 1997.

10 From *Work Rage: Identify the Problems, Implement the*

Solutions, by Gerry Smith. Toronto: HarperCollins Publishers Ltd., 2000, p. 21.

11 In "Time to chill out, Canada," *Globe and Mail,* February 29, 2000.

12 See #9 above, p. 15.

13 From James 4:14. *The NIV Study Bible, 10th Anniversary Edition.* Grand Rapids: The Zondervan Corporation, 1995, p. 1883.

14 In "Cracking the Code of Change," *Harvard Business Review,* May–June 2000.

15 From *A Simpler Way,* by Margaret J. Wheatley and Myron Kellner-Rogers. San Francisco: Berrett-Koehler Publishers, 1996, p. 100.

16 See *The Hungry Spirit, Beyond Capitalism: A Quest for Purpose in the Modern World,* by Charles Handy. New York: Broadway Books, 1998, p. 150.

17 See *Lincoln on Leadership: Executive Strategies for Tough Times,* by Donald T. Phillips. New York: Warner Books, 1992, p. 3.

18 *Ibid.,* p. 137.

19 *Ibid.,* p. 137.

20 See *Blur: The Speed of Change in the Connected Economy,* by Stan Davis and Christopher Meyer. Reading" Addison-Wesley Longman, Inc., 1998, pp. 7–8.

21 From *Thinking in the Future Tense: Leadership Skills for a New Age,* by Jennifer James. New York: Simon & Schuster, 1996, p. 126.

22 See #15 above, p. 251.

23 From "Worker stress costing economy billions, panel warns," by Virginia Galt, *Globe and Mail,* July 21, 2000, p. B9.

24 From "The Internet: What Does It Look Like?" *Fast Company,* March 2000, p. 219. Fast Company's source was Aaron Fischer, "Is Your Career Killing You?" *Data Communications,* February 1998.

25 From *Edgewalkers Weekly Insight,* June 19, 2000.

26 From the *Cluetrain Manifesto: The End of Business as Usual,* by Rick Levine, Christopher Locke, Doc Searls and David Weinberger. Cambridge: Perseus Books, 2000, p. xii.

27 From "The Great Media Shift: Television, Radio and Print in the 21st Century," by Mark Starowicz, First Annual Kesterton Lecture, School of Journalism and Communication, Carleton University, Ottawa, Canada, February 10, 2000.

28 See *The Ultimate Book of Business Quotations,* by Stuart Crainer. New York: Amacom, American Management Association, 1998, p. 58.

29 From *Harvard Business Review on Change.* Boston: Harvard Business School Publishing, 1999, p. 12.

30 From "Workforce Diversity," in *Encyclopedia of the Future,* edited by George Thomas Kurian and Graham T.T. Molitor. New York: Macmillan Library Reference USA, 1996, p. 1006.

31 See #28 above, p. 13.

32 From *Worldwide Laws of Life: 200 Eternal Spiritual Principles,* by John Marks Templeton. Philadelphia: Templeton Foundation Press, 1997, p. 33.

33 From *Dreams of Millennium: Report From a Culture on the Brink,* by Mark Kingwell. Toronto: Penguin Books Canada Ltd., 1996, p. 342.

34 From *Find and Use Your Inner Power,* by Emmet Fox. San Francisco: HarperCollins, 1992, pp. 174–175.

Resources

N o resource list can be complete. This collection lists books, magazines and on-line sources of information the author has found enlightening, interesting and useful for many different projects, including research for *The Living Workplace.*

Books

Abrahamson, Vickie, Mary Meehan, and Larry Samuel. *The Future Ain't What It Used To Be: The 40 Cultural Trends Transforming Your Job, Your Life, Your World.* New York: Riverhead Books, 1997.

Adams, Michael. *Sex in the Snow: Canadian Social Values at the End of the Millennium.* Toronto: Penguin Books Canada Ltd., 1997.

Arbinger Institute, The. *Leadership and Self-Deception: Getting Out of the Box.* San Francisco: Berrett-Koehler Publishers, 2000.

Banks, Robert, and Kimberly Powell (Eds.). *Faith in Leadership: How Leaders Live Out Their Faith in Their Works and Why It Matters.* San Francisco: Jossey-Bass Publishers, 2000.

Barnard, Robert, Dave Cosgrave, and Jennifer Welsh. *Chips & Pop: Decoding the Nexus Generation*. Toronto: Malcolm Lester Books, 1998.

Berlin, Isaiah. *The Proper Study of Mankind*. Pimlico, 1998.

Borsook, Paulina. *Cyberselfish: A Critical Romp Through the Terribly Libertarian Culture of High Tech*. New York: Public Affairs, 2000.

Brandon, Joel, and Daniel Morris. *Just Don't Do It! Challenging Assumptions in Business*. New York: McGraw-Hill, 1997.

Carlton, Richard, PhD *Don't Sweat the Small Stuff . . . and it's all small stuff: Simple Ways to Keep Little Things from Taking Over Your Life*. New York: Hyperion, 1997.

Celente, Gerald. *Trends 2000: How to Prepare for and Profit from the Changes of the 21st Century*. New York: Warner Books, Inc., 1997.

Crainer, Stuart. *The Ultimate Book of Business Quotations*. New York: Amacom, 1998.

Daintith, John *et al.* (Ed.). *Bloomsbury Thematic Dictionary of Quotations*. London: Bloomsbury Publishing Limited, 1988.

Dalla Costa, John. *The Ethical Imperative: Why Moral Leadership is Good Business*. Toronto: HarperCollins Publishers Ltd., 1998.

Davis, Stan, and Christopher Myer. *Blur: The Speed of Change in the Connected Economy*. Reading: Addison-Wesley Longman, Inc., 1998.

Elkington, John. *Cannibals With Forks: The Triple Bottom Line of 21st Century Business*. Gabriola Island: New Society Publishers, 1998.

Fox, Emmet. *Find and Use Your Inner Power*. New York: Harper-Collins Publishers, 1992.

Hamel, Gary, and C.K. Prahalad. *Competing for the Future: Break-through Strategies for Seizing Control of Your Industry and Creating the Markets of Tomorrow*. Boston: Harvard Business School Press, 1994.

Handy, Charles. *The Hungry Spirit: Beyond Capitalism—A Quest for Purpose in the Modern World*. New York: Broadway Books, 1998.

Harvard Business Review on Change. Boston: Harvard Business School Press, 1998.

Imparato, Nicholas, and Oren Harari. *Jumping the Curve: Innovation and Strategic Choice in an Age of Transition*. San Francisco: Jossey-Bass Inc., 1994.

James, Jennifer. *Thinking in the Future Tense: Leadership Skills for a New Age*. New York: Simon & Schuster, 1996.

Jones, Laurie Beth. *Jesus CEO: Using Ancient Wisdom for Visionary Leadership*. New York: Hyperion, 1995.

Kane-Zweber, Kathy, and the Motorola Flexible Work Options Team. *Flexible Work Options: A Guidebook for Employees, Managers, and Human Resource Professionals*. Schaumburg, Illinois: Motorola University Press, 1997.

Kingwell, Mark. *Dreams of Millennium: Report From a Culture on the Brink*. Toronto: Penguin Books Canada Ltd., 1996.

Kostash, Myrna. *The Next Canada: In Search of Our Future Nation*. Toronto: McClelland & Stewart Inc., 2000.

Levine, Rick (Frederick), Christopher Locke, Doc Searls, and David Weinberger. *The Cluetrain Manifesto: The End of Business as Usual*. Cambridge: Perseus Books, 2000.

Lewin, Roger, and Birute Regine. *The Soul at Work: Listen, Respond, Let Go, Embracing Complexity Science for Business Success*. New York: Simon & Schuster, 2000.

Lowe, Graham. *The Quality of Work: A People-Centred Agenda*. Toronto: Oxford University Press, 2000.

Manz, Charles C. *The Leadership Wisdom of Jesus: Practical Lessons for Today*. San Francisco: Berrett-Koehler Publishers, Inc., 1999.

Muggeridge, Malcolm. *A Third Testament*. Toronto: Little, Brown and Company, 1976.

O'Reilly, Charles A. and Jeffrey Pfeffer. *Hidden Value: How Great Companies Achieve Extraordinary Results with Ordinary People.* Boston: Harvard Business School Press, 2000.

Orsborn, Carol. *Inner Excellence: Spiritual Principles of Life-Driven Business.* San Rafael: New World Library, 1992.

Pfeiffer, J. William. *RoadKill on the Information Highway: The Future of Work in Canada.* Toronto: Pfeiffer & Company, 1999.

Phillips, Donald T. *Lincoln on Leadership: Executive Strategies for Tough Times.* New York: Warner Books, Inc., 1992.

Reina, Dennis S., and Michelle L. Reina. *Trust & Betrayal in the Workplace: Building Effective Relationships in Your Organization.* San Francisco: Berrett-Koehler Publishers, 1999.

Scott, Mark Coleridge. *Re-Inspiring the Corporation: The Seven Seminal Paths to Competitive Advantage.* New York: John Wiley & Sons Inc., 2000.

Sennett, Richard. *The Corrosion of Character: The Personal Consequences of Work in the New Capitalism.* New York: W.W. Norton & Company, Inc., 1998.

Smith, Gerry. *Work Rage: Identify the Problems, Implement the Solutions.* Toronto: HarperCollins Publishers Ltd., 2000.

Templeton, John Marks. *Worldwide Laws of Life: 200 Eternal Spiritual Principles.* Radnor: Templeton Foundation Press, 1997.

Tomlinson, Gerald. *Treasury of Religious Quotations.* Englewood Cliffs: Prentice Hall, 1991.

Volf, Miroslav. *Exclusion and Embrace: A Theological Exploration of Identity, Otherness, and Reconciliation.* Nashville: Abingdon Press, 1996.

Wacker Watts and Jim Taylor, with Howard Means. *The Visionary's Handbook: Nine Paradoxes That Will Shape the Future of Your Business.* New York: HarperCollins Publishers, 2000.

Wheatley, Margaret J., and Myron Kellner-Rogers. *A Simpler Way.* San Francisco: Berrett-Koehler Publishers, 1996.

Whyte, David. *The Heart Aroused: Poetry and the Preservation of the Soul in Corporate America*. New York: Doubleday Currency, 1996.

Worzel, Richard. *The Next Twenty Years of Your Life: A Personal Guide into the Year 2017*. Toronto: Stoddart Publishing Co. Limited, 1997.

On-Line Resources

www.strategis.ic.gc.ca. This Government of Canada site provides easy access to international economic analysis and statistical data with links to Statistics Canada, the U.S. Department of Commerce and comparable sources in other parts of the world. It also provides links to Web sites of other levels of government in Canada.

www.addeq.com. Professor Michael Rock defines emotional intelligence as "the aggregate of the strengths and weaknesses of your emotional competencies that influence how you handle yourself and others in coping with the demands and pressures of your business and personal life." This Web site provides information about emotional intelligence and offers an interactive self-assessment and self-study.

www.canadaone.com. CanadaOne provides business-related resources. It offers a monthly magazine, a business directory, an events calendar, a technology center, promotion tools and other resources for Canadian small businesses and entrepreneurs.

www.census.gov The U.S. Census Bureau, United States Department of Commerce, provides demographic information about the U.S.A., publications and links to related sites. Information is organized in broad categories such as people, business, geography, news and special topics.

www.ceoexpress.com. An excellent source for news, research and business information. Includes newsfeeds, statistics, Bartlett's quotations and business links, including chambers of commerce.

www.ctrcorp.com. Computer Technology Research Corp. publishes in-depth e-commerce reports on topics such as client/server communications, information technology management, the Internet, the Web, intranets, extranets and networking. Information is available in English, German, French and Spanish. CTR Corp. also publishes a monthly IT journal that tracks business and technology developments.

www.davinci-institute.com. The Da Vinci Institute is a not-for-profit research and educational institute. Operating as a network of futurists and visionaries, it focuses on emerging technologies. The site's resources include an on-line magazine and links to cutting-edge products and projects.

www.editors-service.com Editors' Service is a small, independent news syndicate that provides quality news products to journalists. The Internet Newsroom is the Editors' Service on-line publication for journalists and other information professionals. The purpose is to help them get quality story material and information from the Internet. This includes names of reliable sources for politics, medicine, business and reference.

www.expoguide.com. EXPOguide, Inc. is an on-line source for comprehensive lists of trade shows and conferences worldwide. It also provides contact information for several industry associations.

www.ftc.gov. The U.S. Federal Trade Commission's Web site provides information and research on legislation, policy and other marketplace issues. Its Business Guidance page has information on various topics, including business opportunities. Its Economic Issues page has economic analyses, working papers and profiles. Other pages deal with job and procurement opportunities, FTC offices and bureaus, and where to go for more information.

www.health.harvard.edu. Harvard Health Publications provides access to health information prepared with the public in mind. The goal is to provide the expertise of Harvard Medical School's faculty and hospital affiliates to individuals so that they are better able to deal with their health care professionals. Resources include books, newsletters and special reports. Many publications are available on-line. Some are provided free; others require a subscription fee.

www.hoovers.com. Hoover's Online: The Business Network is a comprehensive source of business information on companies and industries, money management, career development, news and business travel. The Hoover's Business Directory has sections focusing on industry, news and six other categories. Access to some pages and services is restricted to members. This includes advanced search tools that allow users to sift and sort information and generate customized results.

www.internettrafficreport.com The Internet Traffic Report monitors the flow of data around the world by continent. It displays values between 0 and 100. The higher the number, the more reliable the connections.

www.marketingtools.com. This American Demographics site provides access to *American Demographic* magazine current and back issues, marketing and research tools, and other resources.

www.nlsearch.com. Northern Light Search is an Internet search engine and developer of the world's first *research* engine. The goal is to index and classify human knowledge into a consistent standard and make it available in an integrated form. This site provides access to periodicals and information in various categories. Founded in 1995 in Cambridge, Massachusetts, Northern Light has been praised as providing a wholly original contribution to solving the problem of too much data and too much information by improving the ability of Web searchers to focus on what is relevant and of high quality.

www.prnewswire.com. PR Newswire is a leading source of immediate news from corporations worldwide for media, business, the financial community and individual investors. Visitors may check current news stories or search by topic, such as technology, health/biotech, stock quotes and energy.

www.rileyguide.com. The Riley Guide is a directory of employment and career information sources. Used to see trends in the workplace.

www.sciencemag.org. At this site, the American Association for the Advancement of Science provides *Science* magazine, which has current essays on science and society. The association also provides a news service, supplemental data and other resources. *Science,* the magazine, is available on-line and in print.

www.smartbiz.com. Smartbiz.com is the free, on-line business resource guide on the SBS (Smart Business Supersite) Web site. The SBS site also provides business-related profiles, articles, directories, events listings and special features.

www.statcan.ca. Statistics Canada is Canada's national statistical agency. It provides daily news, economic, social, and census data, educational resources and analyses of statistical releases.

www.templeton.org. The John Templeton Foundation was established in 1987 to encourage a fresh appreciation of the critical importance of the moral and spiritual dimensions in life. A nonprofit grant-making organization, the foundation funds more than 150 projects, studies, award programs and publications around the world.

www.templetonpress.org. The Templeton Foundation Press was founded in 1997 as a program of Templeton Foundation, Inc. Its mission is to publish scholarly and trade books on a variety of subjects, including the connections between science and religion, spirituality and healing in medicine, universal spiritual laws, character development, and freedom.

www.thelivingworkplace.com. Share your workplace observations, comments and stories with Ann Coombs, Thought Leader, Knowledge Navigator, and author of *The Living Workplace.* This site also offers you an opportunity to learn more about the author's work, contact her directly and respond with your views about the future workplace.

www.thestandard.com. The Standard, a San Francisco-based company with offices in New York City, London, Hong Kong, Tokyo and Buenos Aires, specializes in research and information relating to the Internet economy. It publishes a weekly news-magazine, *The Industry Standard,* and offers news, analysis, business intelligence, white papers, case studies, directories, conferences and events on a variety of topics, including Commerce, Culture, Ideas & Strategies, Jobs & Workplace, Media & Marketing, Money & Markets, Policy & Politics, and Tech & Telecom.

www.utnereader.com. The *Utne Reader Online* is described as "a place in cyberspace where ideas and community interest intersect." Founded in 1984, *Utne Reader* reprints articles from more than 2,000 alternative media sources on topics that include technology, society, culture and spirit.

www.wiredwoman.com. The Wired Woman Society is a not-for-profit organization designed to encourage women to explore opportunities in information technology. The Web site provides networking, career resources, community and academic presentations, role modeling and mentoring. For the career and education section of the Web site, select *sugarmomma@wiredwoman.com*

www.worldbank.org. The World Bank Group is an international organization founded in 1944 for the purpose of relieving world poverty. It is known for its economic research, which covers such topics as infrastructure, private sector development, labor and economics, and health and population.

www.wri.org. The World Resources Institute (WRI) is a Washington, D.C.-based educational organization. Its purpose is to respond quickly to emerging environmental issues, and its interests include improving the management of environmental issues by the private sector. As a charitable organization, it is supported by corporate and individual gifts and foundation grants. WRI is a member of Earth Share, which represents some 40 U.S. environment organizations.

Periodicals

The Atlantic Monthly, The Atlantic Monthly Group, 77 N. Washington Street, Boston MA 02114, U.S.A. Tel 617-854-7700. E-mail *custserv@business2.com*.

Business 2.0, Imagine Media, Inc., 150 North Hill Drive, Brisbane CA 94005 U.S.A. Tel 1-800-234-0804. *www.business2.com*.

Canadian Business, Rogers Media, 777 Bay Street, Toronto ON Canada M5W 1A7. Tel 416-596-5100. *www.canadianbusiness.com*

The Economist, Editorial Office, 25 St. James Street, London SW1A 1HG, Tel 44 20 7830 7000. In the U.S.A., The Economist Newspaper, NA, Incorporated, 111 West 57th Street, New York NY 10019-2211. Tel 212-541-0500. *www.economist.com*

Fast Company, Fast Co. Inc., 77 North Washington Street, Boston MA 02114-1927, U.S.A. *www.fastcompany.com*

Forbes, 60 Fifth Avenue, New York NY 10011, U.S.A. Tel 1-800-888-9896. *www.forbes.com*

Fortune, P.O. Box 60001, Tampa FL 33660-0001, U.S.A. Tel 1-800-621-8000. *www.fortune.com*

The Futurist, The World Future Society, 7910 Woodmont Avenue, Suite 450, Bethseda, MD 20814, U.S.A. Toll-free 1-800-989-8274. *www.wfs.org*

Harper's Magazine, Harper's Magazine Foundation, 666 Broadway, New York NY 10012, U.S.A. Tel 212-614-6500. *www.harpers.org*

Harvard Business Review, Harvard Business School Publishing, 60 Harvard Way, Boston MA 02163 U.S.A. Toll-free 1-800-274-3214. *www.hbsp.harvard.edu*

IE: Money, Transcontinental Publishing, 90 Richmond Street East, Suite 100, Toronto ON Canada M5C 1P1. Tel 416-366-4200. *www.iemoney.com*

Ivey Business Journal, Richard Ivey School of Business, 179 John Street, Suite 501, Toronto ON Canada M5T 1X4. *www.ivey.uwo.ca/ibjdemo*

Marketing Magazine, 777 Bay Street, 5th Floor, Toronto ON Canada M5W 1A7. Toll-free 1-800-222-5029. *www.marketing-mag.ca*

Profit: The Magazine for Canadian Entrepreneurs, Rogers Media, 777 Bay Street, 5th Floor, Toronto ON Canada M5W 1A7. Tel 416-596-5999. *www.profitguide.com*

WIRED, Wired Publications Inc., P.O. Box 55690, Boulder CO 80323-5690 U.S.A. Tel 1-800-SO WIRED. *www.wired.com*

Acknowledgments for Copyright Materials

Adapted with permission from *Worldwide Laws of Life: 200 Eternal Spiritual Principles*, Week Thirty-Nine, Law 3, pages 469–471. By John Marks Templeton. Published by Templeton Foundation Press, Philadelphia & London, 1997.

Index

ANN COOMBS   the Living workplace
soul, spirit and success in the 21st century

Unfolding the Possibilities

Thank you for adding *The Living Workplace* to your library. This book is the result of my many years of professional experience as a thought leader, facilitator and strategist. I look forward to hearing about your own experiences in the workplace and welcome your questions, insights and visions.

Ann Coombs, March 2001

Have Ann Coombs...

...address your management team on achieving a living workplace.
...share insights about the consumers of the future and their impact.
...conduct a Working Fearlessly Workshop for your organization.

Coombs Consulting & Associates has, for over 20 years, provided clients with a range of services:

Performance Devolpment Programs • Thinkubators
Trend-spotting excursions • Consumer Research
Graphic Design/Advertising • Service Excellence Surveys

For informaton, please contact:
Coombs Consulting Ltd.
Toronto (416) 483-1411   Vancouver (604) 733-9014
Email: info@coombs.ca
or visit: www.thelivingworkplace.com
